Claire's kitcher

Claire's
kitchen

CLAIRE CAMINADA

Suzanne & George
With best wishes
al happy cooking !
Claire x

18. 9. 10 xox

Contents

All my life I have been surrounded and influenced by people with a love of food, including an inspiring French grandmother who showed me not just the importance of good food, but its role in entertaining – both on a simple and grand scale.

This book has evolved from my passion for food, and a desire to gather together all the recipes I have learned and loved; from my childhood, my student days, my time spent travelling in France, New York and Australia. These are the recipes I have shared with friends and clients alike; some I have created, some have been inspired by food I've tried elsewhere, but all are delicious and easy to cook, and most can be prepared in advance.

Every recipe here is one that I have tried and tested on numerous occasions; I know they all work, and the instructions given here should be easy to follow for even the most inexperienced cook.

So here they are, from my kitchen to yours. I hope you enjoy cooking these recipes and have as much fun with them as I have done and continue to do, whether at a drinks party, a dinner party, a picnic on the beach or a casual catch-up with friends.

Fabulous Finger Food

Canapés, tapas, mezze – call them what you may – are a delicious way to begin an evening – whether at a dinner or drinks party or just an inpromptu gathering of friends or neighbours.

Once the darlings of glittering soirées amongst the smart set, in these modern times canapés have found a new audience as less formal, but no less elegant, 'nibbles' or appetisers. Indeed, by their bite-sized nature they are perfect for popping into the mouth with one hand (a drink in the other, of course!), or to whet, but not spoil, the appetite as an alternative starter before the main event.

The recipes I've included here are the ones that I've found to be most popular amongst everyone I've entertained at home and for clients whose parties I've catered for. Before supper or lunch, allow 3–4 bites per person with 2–3 different savoury recipes that can be prepared ahead and assembled at the last minute. For large numbers (25+) at a drinks party likely to run for about 3–4 hours, choose about 8 recipes: 4 cold, 4 hot and 2 sweet. Be happy knowing there is plenty of food rather than too little; for at the end of a good party 'the munchies' set in for the survivors, and any leftover canapés tend to be polished off.

Marmite and Gruyère palmiers

Marmite – you either love it or hate it. These palmiers started out as a firm favourite for my children's parties, then made with Cheddar, but as they were gobbled up by children and parents alike, I began to serve them at drinks parties – and they are still as popular today as ever. They are extremely easy to assemble and are best served warm at any time of the day. As a sophisticated alternative, these could be made with anchovy paste and sprinkled with sesame seeds.

MAKES 50

375g (13oz) puff pastry

flour, for dusting

Marmite, for spreading

300g (10oz) Gruyère, grated

200g (7oz) mature Cheddar, grated

80g (2½oz) Parmesan, grated

Roll out the pastry on a well-floured, cool surface until it forms a large rectangle. Spread the Marmite evenly right to the edges of the pastry and sprinkle the Gruyère and Cheddar over the top. Beginning from the outside edge, very carefully and tightly roll the pastry inwards; rolling each side alternately until they meet in the middle and resemble an elongated heart shape or palmier. Brush a little extra Marmite where the two rolls meet to seal. Cut the pastry roll in half, wrap each piece in cling film and set aside in the fridge for 1 hour.

Preheat the oven to 190°C/375°F/Gas 5. Remove the cling film and slice the long roll into 6mm-thick slices on the diagonal with a heavy, sharp knife. Lay the pieces on a baking tray lined with baking parchment, spacing them 6cm (2½in) apart, then scatter over the grated Parmesan. Transfer to the oven and bake for about 7 minutes until they are golden brown. Flip them over with a small palate knife and return to the oven for 2 minutes.

Allow to cool on the baking tray for 5 minutes, then carefully transfer them to a large plate and serve.

Caesar tartlets

These attractive, light canapés are simplicity themselves. The filo cases can be made in advance or kept on standby for any unexpected guests; they freeze perfectly (put them in boxes to prevent them being crushed in the freezer) or can be stored in an airtight container in the fridge for 2 weeks. The Caesar dressing can also be used with salad, served with some grilled chicken or salmon.

MAKES 70

140g (5oz) filo pastry sheets

25g (1oz) melted butter

1½ slices white bread

1 Little Gem lettuce

10 hard-boiled quails' eggs
(cooked for 4 minutes)

The dressing

1 egg yolk

1 garlic clove, finely grated

2 tbsp lemon juice

1 tsp anchovy paste

4 tbsp olive oil

100g (3½oz) Parmesan, finely grated

freshly ground black pepper

(this recipe includes raw egg, so do not serve it to vulnerable groups, such as pregnant women and old people)

Preheat the oven to 200°C/400°F/Gas 6. Divide and cut the filo sheets into 5cm squares to make 210 squares. Brush 3 squares with melted butter and arrange them on top of each other at an angle to form a 12-point star. (Cover the rest of the filo sheets with damp kitchen paper and cling film while you do this to prevent them drying out and cracking.) Repeat with the other squares and press each pastry case gently into the wells of three 24-hole, non-stick mini-muffin tins. Cook in the oven for about 8 minutes until they are crisp and golden. Leave the oven on.

Cut the crusts off the bread and cut the slices into tiny cubes. Scatter over a baking tray and bake them in the oven for about 8 minutes or until golden brown. Cut the lettuces into quarters and slice the leaves finely. Peel and quarter the eggs. Set aside until needed.

In a large bowl, whisk together the egg yolk, garlic, lemon juice, anchovy paste and olive oil until well combined. Toss the croutons, lettuce and grated Parmesan into the dressing. You will probably need only half of the dressing, put the rest in the fridge to use for a salad

Anything up to an hour before serving, fill the tartlets with the salad mixture and top each with a quails' egg and a grinding of black pepper.

Chilli and rosemary nuts

A spicy selection of mixed nuts is ideal for keeping on hand for whenever you need something to serve alongside drinks. These can be stored in an airtight container for up to 2 months.

**MAKES ENOUGH TO FILL
A 1-LITRE CONTAINER**

100g (3½oz) Brazil nuts

100g (3½oz) shelled pistachio nuts

100g (3½oz) raw cashews

100g (3½oz) hazelnuts

100g (3½oz) almonds

80g (2½oz) unsalted butter

2 tbsp muscovado sugar

1 tsp cayenne powder

2 tsp rock salt

3 sprigs of fresh rosemary

Preheat the oven to 200°C/400°F/Gas 6. Tip all the nuts onto a baking tray and warm them in the oven for 5 minutes.

Put the butter, sugar, cayenne and salt in a large frying pan and gently cook, without stirring, until the butter has melted and the sugar dissolved.

Meanwhile, strip the rosemary leaves off their stalks and chop finely. Bring the caramel mixture to the boil and stir in the rosemary and warmed nuts. Continue to cook for a further 5 minutes, stirring occasionally, then turn off the heat. Allow the nuts to completely cool in the pan, then serve or transfer them to an airtight container for storage.

BLT toasties

Living and cooking in the Big Apple meant we were exposed to some classic American favourites, and this bacon/lettuce/tomato variation was one I discovered in the converted tenement of the Tribeca Grand Hotel, Soho. I remember them being especially popular with the hordes of size-o models at the fashion shows we catered for!
The toasted cases can be made a week before and kept in an airtight container, and the filling can be made the day before, then mixed on the day of eating.

MAKES 40

1 loaf thin- or medium-sliced white bread

2 x 250g (9oz) streaky bacon

600g (1lb 5oz) cherry tomatoes

3 Little Gem lettuce, quartered lengthways

3 tbsp full-fat mayonnaise (bought, such as Hellmann's, is fine)

splash of Tabasco, to taste

salt and freshly ground black pepper

Preheat the oven to 200°C/400°F/Gas 6. Roll over the slices of bread with a rolling pin until they are thin enough to line the holes in small tartlet tins, then cut out 40 rounds from each slice using a 3cm (1in) diameter round cutter. Mould the rounds into the tins and bake in the oven until just golden. Leave to cool in the tin, then remove and set aside until needed.

Chop the bacon finely and fry it until it is very crispy. Remove from the frying pan with a slotted spoon and transfer to a plate covered with kitchen paper and leave to cool for 10 minutes.

Chop the tomatoes finely and place in a sieve over a bowl to drain away any excess juice. Finely slice the lettuce quarters, place in a colander then rinse under a cold running tap. Leave to drain.

Mix the bacon and tomato with the mayonnaise, and add some Tabasco, salt and black pepper to taste. Half an hour before needed, fill each of the bread toasties with a small pinch of lettuce and top with the tomato and bacon mix.

Toasted brioche with Thai-style tuna tartare

Classic Thai flavourings give these tuna bites a delicious and refreshing edge. They are quick and easy to put together and are always extremely popular. Use the freshest sushi-grade tuna you can buy, and use it on the day it is bought. Do not marinade the tuna for more than 1 hour or the fish will overcook in the acidity of the lime juice. If you can't get tuna, very fresh halibut or wild salmon makes a good alternative.

MAKES 24 BITES

450g (1lb) fresh sushi-grade tuna

1 brioche or sweet bread loaf, sliced into 2cm (¾in) slices

fresh chervil sprigs or chopped chives, to garnish

The marinade

small bunch of coriander, finely chopped

1 tbsp fresh mint, finely chopped

1 small green chilli, finely chopped

1 large garlic clove, finely chopped

zest and juice of 2 limes

1 tbsp fish sauce

1 tbsp good sesame oil

splash of Tabasco, to taste

Combine all the marinade ingredients then check for seasoning, adding more fish sauce, sesame oil or Tabasco to taste, if you wish. Roughly chop the tuna into small 1cm chunks and toss in the marinade. Set aside in the fridge for 1 hour to absorb all the wonderful flavours.

Preheat the oven to 200°C/400°F/Gas 6. Cut out little circles from the brioche using 3cm-diameter round cutters. Set them on a baking tray and toast very briefly in the oven until they are just golden on both sides.

Just before serving, mould a teaspoon of the tuna mix on top of each piece of brioche and garnish with a sprig of chervil or a few chopped chives.

Sourdough toasts with anchovies and shallots

Despite the supposed myth that many people dislike anchovies, these seem to be a perennial favourite. The combination of flavours is fantastic; the chilled unsalted butter diminishes the saltiness of the anchovies, and the finishing touch of a peppery sliver of shallot lingers deliciously.

Use the best anchovies possible (Spanish Ortiz or Tesco's finest are good). I like to prepare the butter and shallots in the morning and leave them in the fridge until needed. Opened jars of anchovies will keep in the fridge for months and the sourdough bread and butter can be kept in the freezer for last-minute use.

MAKES 40

250g good-quality unsalted Normandy butter

4 shallots, very finely sliced

1 tbsp milk

1 loaf of sliced sourdough bread (Poilane is a good French brand)

250g good anchovy fillets in extra virgin oil

freshly ground black pepper

1 lemon and 1 lime, cut into wedges

Slice the butter into 40cm squares approximately ½cm (¼in) thick, then set aside in the fridge. Place the sliced shallots in a dish with the milk and leave to rest in the fridge for 1 hour.

When ready to serve, toast the sliced bread until just warm and cut into 40 x 2cm rough triangular shapes. (Remove any over-toasted crusts.) Drain the shallots from the milk. Set a pat of butter on each piece of toast, top with a few slivers of the shallot and finally a curled anchovy fillet.

Arrange the toasts on a plate and serve with a grinding of black pepper and wedges of fresh lemon and lime.

Caramelised onion and feta tartlets

These tartlets are slightly time consuming to make, but the effort pays dividends because they are so delicious and always a favourite at any party. It is well worth making your own tartlet cases, as bought pastry cases are a poor second to homemade ones. Fresh pastry is so easy to make in the blender and the cut-out cases can be kept in the freezer, cooked or uncooked, in covered trays, or in an airtight container in the fridge for a month. If you don't like feta, replace it with goat's cheese.

MAKES 60

300g (10oz) plain flour,
plus extra for dusting

60g (2oz) strong Cheddar cheese

120g (4½oz) salted butter

pinch each of cayenne and
mustard powder

450g (1lb) large red onions,
finely chopped

284ml pot double cream

125g (4½oz) Greek or Lebanese
feta cheese

small tin of pitted black olives

6 SunBlush or sundried tomatoes

salt and freshly ground black pepper

3 tbsp chopped fresh basil

Place the flour, cheese and 80g (2½oz) of the butter in a blender with the cayenne and mustard powders. Process until the mixture forms fine crumbs. With the motor running, add enough cold water so that the crumbs form a large ball of dough. Remove to a plate and set aside to rest in the fridge for 20 minutes.

Melt the remaining butter in a large frying pan, add the onions and cook over a medium heat for about 15 minutes, stirring occasionally, until the mixture begins to caramelize. Add the cream, bring to the boil, then simmer for 10 minutes until the liquid has reduced, stirring occasionally. Remove from the heat, season to taste and cool.

Preheat the oven to 200°C/400°F/Gas 6. Roll out the pastry thinly on a lightly floured surface. Stamp out rounds with a floured 5cm diameter cutter and line three 24-hole, non-stick tartlet trays with the pastry. Prick the bases with a fork and chill in the fridge for half an hour. Place a scrunched ball of foil in each case to cover the pastry and bake in the oven for about 10 minutes until golden brown (this is known as blind baking).

Remove the pastry cases from their tins and set out on a flat baking tray. Stir the feta into the onion mixture while warm. Fill each pastry case with a generous teaspoonful of the mixture, then top with a slice of olive, some tomato and a pinch of basil. Return the tartlets to the oven and cook for 10 minutes. Allow to cool for 5 minutes before serving.

Chicken and lemongrass skewers

A delicious favourite with a fragrant twist. If you want to get ahead, the chicken can be marinated up to 2 days before cooking, then be parcooked in the oven and finished off just before serving. As a variation, strips of pork fillet or butterflied king prawns could be substituted for the chicken.

MAKES 30

5 large skinless and boneless chicken breasts

12 plump spring onions, trimmed and cut into 2cm diagonal pieces

The marinade

1½ tbsp runny honey

4 tbsp dark soy sauce

3 tbsp sake or sherry

3 tbsp sesame oil

6 lemongrass stems, soft white centre finely chopped

2 shallots, finely chopped

Mix all the marinade ingredients together. Slice the chicken fillets into even 1cm slices and toss well in the marinade to coat. Cover and chill for 2 hours to allow the flavours to infuse the meat. If using wooden skewers, soak thirty 12cm (5in) skewers in water for 30 minutes to prevent them burning.

Preheat the oven to 180°C/350°F/Gas 4. Assemble the skewers by first threading the spring onion pieces onto the drained skewers, followed by chicken, alternating them as you go so that there are 2 pieces of chicken on each skewer. Cover a baking tray with foil, set the skewers on the tray and cook for 5 minutes on each side until the chicken is cooked through.

Hoisin duck pancakes

The filling for these pancake treats can be prepared the day before and kept, covered, in the fridge until needed. However, do not assemble the pancakes more than 2 hours in advance, otherwise they will turn soggy. Chinese pancakes can be found in any good Asian supermarket; I keep some in the freezer and prise them apart as needed.

MAKES 24

2 large duck breasts, skin on

1 tsp ground cloves

12 spring onions

½ cucumber

hoisin sauce

12 Chinese pancakes

Lay the duck breast skin-side down and trim off any excess fat. Using a sharp knife, score across the top fat and sprinkle it with the ground cloves. Heat a frying pan over a high flame and cook the duck breasts, skin-side down, in the hot pan. Cook for about 7 minutes on each side, until they are springy to the touch and not too pink in the centre. Remove from the pan and set aside on some kitchen paper to absorb any excess oil.

Trim the ends of the spring onions and cut the stems in half. Finely slice them lengthways until you are left with long slivers of onion. Peel the cucumber and cut into lengths equal to those of the spring onions. Remove the seeds with a sharp knife and finely slice the flesh until you are left with fine slivers.

Slice the duck breasts thinly and then again into thin strips. Cover with just enough hoisin sauce to bind the duck pieces together.

Cut the pancakes in half, spoon a little duck on the centre of each, then set the spring onion and cucumber slivers so they are just hanging over the rounded edge of the pancake. Carefully roll the pancakes into a tight cone. Place the filled pancakes in a dish, tightly packed together. Cover and set aside, then serve arranged on a white platter.

Thai fish cakes

These fish cakes are extremely quick and easy to make and can be eaten as canapés or made larger and eaten as part of a main course. Any fish can be used as long as it is fairly firm and has had all of its bones removed. I like to sauté the fish cakes ahead of time so as not have any fish or frying smells in the house when people arrive, then set them in a low oven to warm through before serving. They are delicious served with a dollop of Thai sweet chilli sauce, lime aioli, lime Hollandaise or a Quick coriander and lime tartare sauce (see page 153).

SERVES 40

300g (10oz) firm white fish fillet, skinned and cut into chunks

1 large tbsp red curry paste

1 egg

1 tbsp fish sauce

1 tsp caster sugar

1 tbsp cornflour

1 tbsp finely chopped coriander (including stalks)

2 lemongrass stalks, peeled and finely chopped

zest and juice of 2 limes

coarse soughdough or Panko breadcrumbs

salt and freshly ground black pepper

vegetable oil, for frying

In a blender, process all the ingredients up to the breadcrumbs. Mould the mix between your thumb and index finger into small, round, slightly flattened patties. Put the breadcrumbs on a plate, season them and roll the cakes in the breadcrumbs so that they are lightly and evenly coated. Chill for 1 hour.

Heat a little oil in a large frying pan until very hot and carefully add the fish cakes to the pan. Sauté for about 3 minutes on one side, then carefully turn them over and cook for a further 3 minutes on the other side until golden – do not undercook them or they will fall apart when picked up. Remove from the pan and set on kitchen paper to absorb any excess oil. Serve warm, topped with your chosen relish.

Walnut and goat's cheese sables

In French, sable means sand, and these delicious, crumbly, shortbread-type biscuits have just that sort of texture. They can be topped with many flavours other than walnuts and goat's cheese – salsa verde, a sprig of rocket with Parmesan shavings, some chunky homemade pesto, or perhaps an oven-roasted cherry tomato make delicious variations. Keep a batch in the freezer so that you can dig them out to serve for those impromptu guests, or serve them slightly warm with drinks before dinner.

MAKES ABOUT 40

150g (5½oz) plain flour, plus extra for dusting

pinch each of salt, mustard powder and cayenne pepper

150g (5½oz) lightly salted butter, chilled and cubed

150g (5½oz) strong Cheddar, finely grated

80g (3oz) crumbled goat's cheese

80g (3oz) walnuts, chopped

Using a blender, process the flour, salt, mustard powder and cayenne briefly. Add the cubed butter and pulse until the mixture becomes the consistency of breadcrumbs. Add the grated Cheddar and blend again until it comes together as a large dough ball.

On a well-floured surface, roll out the pastry until it is 2cm (¾in) thick, then stamp out 2.5cm (1in) bite-sized rounds. Transfer the pastry circles to a non-stick baking tray and set aside to chill in the fridge for 1 hour.

Preheat the oven to 200°C/400°F/Gas 6. Mix together the goat's cheese and walnuts and sprinkle a little of the mixture on top of each sable. Bake for about 10 minutes, until golden brown, then set aside to cool for 5 minutes before removing them from the baking tray to a plate. Serve at room temperature.

Parmesan and thyme crisps

SERVES 20

1kg (2¼lb) Parmesan, grated
large bunch of fresh thyme
freshly ground black pepper

These can be quickly prepared and cooked; the only slightly time consuming part is pulling the leaves off the thyme stalks – although you could use poppy seeds instead. For something special, top them with some very finely sliced rare beef, fresh rocket leaves and a little white truffle oil. These delicious nibbles also work beautifully as a topping to most thick, winter vegetable soups.

Place the Parmesan in a medium-sized mixing bowl and gently pull the thyme leaves off each stalk over the bowl. Mix well to combine and add a grinding of black pepper.

Preheat the oven to 200°C/400°F/Gas 6. Line several baking trays with greaseproof paper and dot heaped teaspoons of the cheese mixture all over, allowing enough room between each mound for them to expand on cooking. Place in the oven and bake for about 6 minutes until they are bubbling and just beginning to brown.

Remove from the oven and set aside to cool for a minute. Carefully prise each crisp off the baking trays using a palate knife, and serve.

Baked artichoke and Parmesan dip

SERVES 8

400g (14oz) artichokes in brine, rinsed and well drained

300g (10oz) Parmesan, roughly grated, plus 100g (3½oz) extra for sprinkling

juice of ½ lemon

2 tbsp mayonnaise
(bought, such as Hellmann's, is fine)

2 garlic cloves, finely chopped

splash of Tabasco, to taste

salt and freshly ground black pepper

1 medium sourdough loaf, sliced and warmed

Charlie and I discovered this magical combination of ingredients in one of our all-time favourite restaurants – Freemans – when we were living in New York, and I adapted it to eat at home as a canapé or starter with slices of warm bread. It is also delicious dolloped into a baked potato. If you want to get ahead, the dip can be made a few days in advance and any leftovers can be heated again.

Place all the ingredients in a blender and pulse to chop the artichokes and combine everything. Check the seasoning and add more Tabasco, lemon juice, salt and pepper to taste,

if needed. Spoon the mixture into a shallow ovenproof dish, sprinkle with the extra 100g (3½oz) Parmesan and set aside in the fridge to chill for a few hours.

Preheat the oven to 180°C/350°F/Gas 4. Set the dish in the centre of the oven and cook for 50–60 minutes until it is bubbling and golden on the top.

Allow the artichoke dip to cool to room temperature, then serve it alongside warm bread for guests to help themselves to.

Pea blinis with lobster and pancetta topping

MAKES 160

The blinis

½ x 400g tin of peas, drained
(French have the best flavour)

110g 4oz) plain flour

1½ tsp baking powder

¼ tsp salt

1 egg, beaten

250ml (9fl oz) milk

freshly ground black pepper

small bunch of mint leaves,
finely chopped

1 tsp sunflower oil

The topping

125g (4½oz) thin pancetta slices

125g (4½oz) mascarpone

1 tbsp chopped chives

125g (4½oz) cooked lobster,
crayfish or cooked peeled prawns

2 tsp finely chopped chives

Perfect make-ahead party nibbles; these blinis can be made a week or so in advance and warmed gently when needed, or even frozen for up to 3 months. These are just as good served as slightly larger blinis for a starter. They are also very pretty!

Place the peas in a blender and pulse to roughly crush them. Place the flour in a large bowl, stir in the baking powder and salt and make a well in the middle. In a separate bowl, mix the eggs with the milk, then slowly pour the liquid into the well, beating all the time. Continue to beat briskly to create a smooth batter, then add the peas, mint and season. Set aside for 10 minutes.

Heat a little of the oil in large frying pan; and once hot, add teaspoons of batter to the pan to form 2.5cm bite-sized rounds. Cook until bubbles begin to appear, then carefully turn them over and continue to cook for a further 2 minutes. Remove with a slotted spoon and drain on kitchen paper.

Fry the pancetta slices until very crisp, and meanwhile beat together the mascarpone and chives until smooth and well combined. Top each blini with a generous spoonful of the mascarpone mixture, set a little lobster, crayfish or a prawn on top and finish off with a couple of broken crispy pancetta slices and a few chives.

Prune and Cognac tartlets

For that end-of-drinks-party sweetness, these are elegant finales. These tarts can also be made as one classic French dessert (a 30cm (12in), deep, loose-bottomed tart tin serves 8, and needs 10 minutes added to the baking time). This combination is delicious and always receives rave reviews.

MAKES 40

400g (14oz) plain flour, plus extra for dusting

pinch of salt

200g (7z) unsalted butter, chilled and cut into cubes

1 tbsp refined golden sugar

1 egg yolk

1 tsp vanilla extract

300g (10oz) good-quality, plump, pitted prunes (Agen ideally)

2 eggs

1 tsp vanilla extract

120g (4½oz) refined golden caster sugar

125g (4½oz) ground almonds

300ml (10fl oz) double cream

zest of 1 lemon

30g (1oz) unsalted butter, melted and cooled

200ml (7fl oz) good cognac or Armagnac

Put the flour and salt in a food processor and whiz for a minute or two. Add the butter and process until the mixture resembles breadcrumbs. Add the sugar, egg yolk and vanilla extract and, with the motor running slowly, pour in a very small amount of chilled water until the mixture comes together in a ball. Wrap the ball in cling film and set aside to rest in the fridge for 20 minutes.

Roll out the dough evenly on a well-floured surface until the pastry is 5mm (¼in) thick. Using a 6cm (2½in) diameter circular cutter, cut out 40 rounds and transfer to two lightly greased, 24-hole mini-muffin tins, pressing the pastry firmly into the moulds. Set in the fridge for a further 30 minutes. Soak the prunes in hot water for 20 minutes. Preheat the oven to 180°C/350°F/Gas 4.

In a large bowl, blend the eggs, vanilla extract, sugar, almonds, cream and lemon zest. Whisk together lightly and add the melted butter. Drain the prunes, cut them up roughly and put a few pieces in each pastry case. Set the muffin tins on baking trays, to catch any spillage, then pour the custard mix into each tart. Cook the tarts in the centre of the oven for 20 minutes until they are golden brown and puffed up.

Remove from the oven and, while still warm, spoon a little cognac over each tartlet. Cool to room temperature.

Macademia and white chocolate chip cookies

Delicious but different chocolate-chip cookies that freeze perfectly. If you can't get macadamias, use unsalted cashew nuts instead. Take care not to overcook the cookies, as they are at their best when they are soft and chewy.

MAKES 70 (SMALL)

175g (6oz) softened unsalted butter

175g (6oz) soft refined golden caster sugar

2 eggs, beaten, at room temperature

125g (4½oz) porridge oats

250g (9oz) plain flour

1 tsp baking powder

250g (9oz) good-quality white chocolate, broken into small chunks

250g (9oz) macadamias, roughly chopped

In a food processor, blend the butter and sugar until pale and fluffy. Gradually add the eggs, a little at a time, blending all the while. Add the oats, flour and baking powder and process thoroughly. Scoop out the mixture with a spatula and transfer to a large bowl. Stir in the chocolate and nuts.

Preheat the oven to 180°C/350°F/Gas 4 and line two baking trays with greaseproof paper. Drop spoonfuls of dough onto the baking trays and flatten them slightly, allowing plenty of room for the cookies to expand. Bake for 10 minutes until golden.

Remove from the oven, leave to cool for a few minutes, then carefully transfer the cookies to a wire rack and leave to cool completely.

Gooey lemon squares

These lemon squares are the fastest and easiest of all cakes to make, because the main work can be done in a blender. As with most sponge cakes, this recipe freezes beautifully too. Should you want to make this as one big cake, just grease and line a loaf tin in the same way and add 10 minutes to the baking time.

MAKES 40 SQUARES

butter for greasing

115g (4oz) unsalted butter

175g (6oz) refined golden caster sugar

175g (6oz) self-raising flour

1 tsp baking powder

2 large eggs

finely grated zest of 2 lemons

75ml (2½fl oz) milk

Syrup

4 tbsp icing sugar

juice and zest of 2 large lemons

Grease and line a 30 x 20cm (12 x 8in) baking tin with greaseproof paper. Preheat the oven to 180°C/350°F/Gas 4.

Whisk all the cake ingredients in a blender, then pour into the tin and bake for 30 minutes until risen. Test by inserting a skewer into the centre of the cake – it should come out clean.

Combine the syrup ingredients and whisk until smooth. Leaving the warm cake still in its tin, prick the sponge all over with a skewer and pour over the syrup. Leave in the tin until completely cooled so it soaks up all the syrup. Remove from the tin and carefully peel off the greaseproof paper. Set on a board and cut into 2.5cm (1in) square bites.

Almond and raspberry roulades

The slight crunch of almond combined with juicy, sweet raspberries and cream make this a colourful and wonderfully light bite that will satisfy any sweet craving. These mini roulades can be prepared up to 2 days ahead and stored in the fridge, or they can be frozen.

SERVES 40

4 eggs

125g (4½oz) refined caster sugar

few drops of almond essence

125g (4½oz) ground almonds

1 tsp baking powder

100g (3½oz) flaked golden almonds

300ml (10fl oz) whipping cream

125g (4½oz) fresh raspberries

Line a Swiss roll tin with baking parchment. Separate the eggs into two large, clean bowls. Whisk the whites in one bowl with half the sugar until they are stiff. In the other bowl, beat together the egg yolks, remaining sugar and almond essence until the mixture is thick and pale in colour.

Preheat the oven to 190°C/375°F/Gas 5. Fold the egg whites, ground almonds and baking powder into the yolk mix and spread evenly over the base of the lined tin. Bake for 20 minutes until just firm to the touch.

Remove from the oven and cut a second large piece of baking parchment and place it on a flat work surface. Sprinkle the paper with the flaked almonds and carefully invert the tin to turn out the roulade onto the nuts. Remove the baking parchment on the base of the sponge then roll it up carefully and tightly along the long edges, using the paper to help you. Set aside to cool.

Whip the cream until thick, then unroll the roulade and cut the rectangle into three evenly sized pieces. Spread each piece with the cream and dot over the raspberries. Roll up each piece as before and wrap tightly in cling film. Set aside in the fridge for at least 2 hours, then slice horizontally into bite-size slices 2cm (¾in) thick.

Treacle tartlets

Perfect tartlets with lots of luscious treacle and a hint of ginger. (This same quantity could also be made as one tart to serve 8 using a 28cm (11in) deep, loose-bottomed tart tin – just add an extra 5 minutes to the cooking times and bake at 200°C/400°F/Gas 6 and then 180°C/350°F/Gas 4.) Whether large or small, the tarts can be made up to 3 days in advance and kept in the fridge. Serve warm with cream, crème fraiche, clotted cream or a good vanilla ice cream.

MAKES 40

For the pastry

140g (5oz) cold butter, cubed, plus extra for greasing

300g (10oz) plain flour, plus extra for greasing

pinch salt

pinch of ground ginger

2 tsp refined sugar

3–4 tbsp cold water

For the filling

75g (2½oz) butter

600g (1lb 5oz) golden syrup (a squeezy bottle is easiest)

5 tbsp double cream

zest and juice of 1 lemon

¼ tsp ground ginger

180g (6oz) white breadcrumbs

Grease two 24-hole muffin tins.

Blend the flour, salt, ginger and sugar in the food processor, then add the butter and whiz until it resembles fine breadcrumbs. Add enough of the cold water to bind the dough. Transfer to a cool, floured work surface, roll out and cut out forty 6cm (2½in) rounds. Line each mould with the pastry circles and place them in the fridge for 30 minutes to prevent the pastry shrinking further.

Meanwhile, make the filling. Melt the butter in a pan set over a medium heat for a few minutes, watching it carefully, until it turns a light golden brown. (This is a beurre noisette.) Set aside.

Preheat the oven to 200°C/400°F/Gas 6. Put all but 2 tablespoons of golden syrup in a pan over a low heat until it dissolves to a liquid. Stir in the cream, beurre noisette, lemon zest and juice, ginger and breadcrumbs. Warm gently for 5 minutes. Fill each tart with a generous teaspoon of filling, then squeeze the remaining syrup over each tart. Bake for 10 minutes, and then lower the oven to 180°C/350°F/Gas 4 and bake for a further 10 minutes. Leave to cool in the tin.

Lazy lunches &
simple suppers

In our fast-paced modern world there are some days when you just want to step back and linger over a delicious and dead-easy meal, catching up on gossip with the girls or news from friends. For these small, casual gatherings you need a slightly different approach; delicious food is a must, of course, but simplicity is key.

A lazy lunch needs to be thrown together without taking all morning, and a supper must be so simple it can be out on the table quickly at the end of a busy day. The best way to achieve this is by a little thought and planning. Advance cooking allows more time for the banter that any gathering of good friends creates. Nearly all the recipes in this chapter can be prepared ahead – in part or in full – and be finished off as your guests settle down with a good drink.

Mix and match these recipes to cater for all seasons, times of day and good diet intentions (!); there are warming soups, satisfying risottos, light and healthy salads and – the perfect end to any casual gathering – deliciously decadent sweet treats. Now there's no excuse for not catching up with friends!

Crab and apple bisque

I first tried something similar to this when I was living in Sydney, Australia, and I just love the combination of apple, spices and crab. This is my version, which is simply delicious served with chunks of warm ciabatta or focaccia.

SERVES 8

2 tbsp butter

2 onions, finely chopped

2 garlic cloves, crushed

2 large Granny Smith apples, peeled and finely grated

2 tbsp curry powder

2 pinches of turmeric

2 tsp cumin

3 tbsp cornflour

1 x 400g tin chopped tomatoes

2 x 500ml good-quality chicken stock

280g (10oz) good-quality white crab meat

300ml (10fl oz) single cream

a few drops of Tabasco

salt and freshly ground black pepper and fino sherry, to taste

sprigs of chervil or coriander, to garnish

Melt the butter in a heavy-based pan and sauté the onions and garlic until transparent. Add the apples, curry powder, turmeric, cumin and cornflour, stirring well. Slowly add the tomatoes and chicken stock, stirring constantly to eliminate any lumps. Bring this to the boil and add the crab meat, cream and seasonings. Check the seasoning and serve in warm bowls garnished with sprigs of chervil or coriander.

Bouillabaisse

I love any opportunity to visit a good fish market when I am abroad, and this hearty soup has been adapted from another well-used and popular recipe we ate as children with my grandmother in Valbonne, and from the years of living in Sydney where I discovered and experimented with a whole new kettle of fish.

The Saffron aioli (see page 156) and vegetable base of the soup can be made in advance. The fish used can vary – depending on your budget and what is fresh and available – however, it should be a meaty variety that will hold its shape once cooked, such as gurnard, monkfish, cod, rock salmon, swordfish or lobster.

Heat the olive oil in a large heavy pan over a medium heat, add the garlic and vegetables and cook gently until they are softened. Add the wine, stock and tomatoes and bring to the boil. Reduce the heat, cover the pan and cook for 20 minutes. Add the lemon juice, sugar and seasoning.

Just before serving, add the fish and cook for about 5 minutes until just tender, then add the scallops, prawns and clams. Cover with a lid, turn off the heat and leave to rest for 5 minutes before serving with a large spoon of aioli and some dill scattered over.

SERVES 8

2 tbsp olive oil

3 garlic cloves, finely chopped

2 medium onions, finely chopped

1 red pepper, finely chopped

1 fennel bulb, finely chopped

1 potato, peeled and chopped

4 ripe plum tomatoes, roughly chopped

150ml (5fl oz) white wine

900ml (1½ pints) fish stock

3 x 400g tins chopped tomatoes

juice of 1 lemon

2 tsp sugar

salt and cayenne pepper

500g (1lb 2oz) monkfish tail, skinned and sliced into large cubes

8 king scallops

16 raw king prawns, shelled and deveined

12 cherrystone clams, razor clams or mussels, cleaned

1 bunch of chopped fresh dill

Chilled cucumber and minted yoghurt soup

This is a great soup for a warm summer, and if you like you can add some fresh shellfish (lobster, crayfish, prawns) to make it really special. This soup is best made a day in advance and kept in the fridge to allow the fragrant flavours to infuse and to chill it nicely.

SERVES 6

2 cucumbers, peeled, cut lengthways into quarters and deseeded

2 garlic cloves, roughly chopped

½ tsp pureed lemongrass or the finely chopped white centre

1 tsp ground cumin

1 tbsp fresh coriander, roughly chopped

1 tbsp mint, roughly chopped

juice of 1 lime

salt and freshly ground black pepper

To finish

1 x 400ml tin coconut milk

500ml (16fl oz) Greek yoghurt

1 tbsp cumin seeds

sesame oil, to serve

chopped chives, to serve

Roughly chop the cucumber pieces and place all the ingredients except those needed to finish in a bowl and leave in the fridge to marinate for 4 hours or ideally overnight. Chill 6 bowls to serve the soup in.

Tip the marinated ingredients into a liquidiser with the coconut milk and yoghurt and purée until fine. Adjust the seasoning and pass the soup through a coarse sieve. Add a few ice cubes and chill in the fridge until needed. Toast the cumin seeds in a dry frying pan and set aside to cool.

Serve the soup in the chilled bowls, drizzled with a little sesame oil and scattered with some chopped chives and tiny pinch of the toasted cumin seeds.

Creamy butternut squash soup

A delicious, colourful, creamy soup for all seasons. Serve with Parmesan thyme crisps (see page 24) or scattered with some roasted mixed spices for extra flavour.

Melt the butter in a large pan and gently cook the onions, garlic and ginger until soft. Add the pumpkin and potato and cook for a few more minutes. Add the wine and boil until the liquid has almost evaporated.

Add the stock and bouquet garni, cover, and gently cook for about 30 minutes until all the vegetables are just soft. Transfer the soup to a liquidiser and blend until smooth.

Lightly toast the spices in a frying pan and pulse them briefly in a grinder to release the flavours, taking care not to over-grind them, or use a pestle and mortar.

Pour the soup into a pan, add the cream and seasonings and gently reheat. Serve sprinkled with a pinch of the warm toasted spices.

SERVES 8

40g (1½oz) butter

3 medium onions, peeled and chopped

2 garlic cloves, crushed

3cm (1in) piece of root ginger, peeled and finely sliced

2 medium butternut pumpkins, peeled and chopped

2 medium potatoes, peeled and chopped

300ml (10fl oz) dry white wine

2 x 750ml cartons good-quality chicken or vegetable stock

1 bouquet garni

1 tsp each of ground coriander, cumin seeds and whole cloves

½ cinnamon stick, broken in half

350ml (12fl oz) double cream

1 tsp jerk seasoning

freshly grated nutmeg, to taste

salt and freshly ground black pepper

Smoked salmon tortinos

These will go down as the most popular starter I served in the 1990s, and they are still much requested. They are also perfect for parties, made in miniature tart tins and served as canapés. The oregano can be substituted with tarragon, if you prefer, and you could use thick soured cream instead of crème fraîche. Serve with a watercress, chicory,orange and avocado salad.

SERVES 8

1 packet filo pastry (about 16 sheets)

150g (5½oz) melted butter

900g (2lb) tinned chopped tomatoes, drained through a sieve

2 tbsp freshly chopped oregano

sea salt and freshly ground black pepper

8 tbsp crème fraîche

640g (1lb 6oz) sliced smoked salmon, cut into strips

1 bunch of fresh dill

Lemon-flavoured olive oil (page 149)

Preheat the oven to 200°C/400°F/Gas 6 and lightly grease 8 fluted, loose-bottomed 12cm (5in) tart tins.

Unroll the filo pastry and cover with cling film and damp kitchen paper. Take one sheet of pastry at a time and brush with melted butter, then cover with another pastry sheet. Repeat this process until the pile is 4 sheets thick. Using a round cutter or a bowl slightly larger than the tart tin, cut out a round from the pastry layers and set it into one tin. Repeat the process until 8 tins are lined.

Put a large tablespoon of the drained tomatoes over the base of each pastry case. Sprinkle generously with fresh oregano and salt and pepper. Cook in the oven for about 8 minutes or until golden. Push the loose bottom from each tart upwards through the centre of each tin and remove the sides. Carefully slide the crispy filo case off its base onto a baking tray.

Add a large tablespoon of crème fraîche to each tart and cook them in a hot oven for about 3 minutes so that the cream bubbles. Remove from the oven and carefully slide them onto individual plates. (They may be cooled and frozen at this stage.) Set the smoked salmon strips and sprigs of dill over the top of each tart. Finish with a little lemon olive oil and serve.

Beetroot carpaccio with herring and new potato tian

I just love beets and their varying colours, and roasting them gives them a much more intense colour and flavour, and also retains all their wonderful nutrients. They can be baked well ahead and stored in the fridge for a week, covered in a little olive oil. Beetroots are perfect partners with a variety of cheeses, particularly in a salad (such as goat or dolcelatte), but I love them with this underused fish, herring.

SERVES 8

1kg (2¼lbs) small raw beetroots

400g (14oz) new potatoes, scrubbed clean

600g (1lb 5oz) pickled herring, drained and finely diced

1 Granny Smith apple, peeled and cored

2 tsp strong horseradish sauce

1 tbsp Greek yoghurt

2 tbsp thick crème fraîche

juice of ½ lemon

2 tbsp chopped chives

salt and freshly ground black pepper

3 tbsp good-quality extra virgin olive oil

1 tbsp red wine vinegar

2 medium shallots, peeled and finely chopped

1 tbsp finely chopped parsley

1 tbsp finely chopped tarragon

160g (5½oz) mixed baby leaf herb salad

Preheat the oven to 160°C/325°F/Gas 3. Trim the beets, leaving a 2.5cm (1in) stem, and rinse well. Set them in a roasting tin with 5mm (¼in) water and cover it with foil. Cook in the oven for 1 hour. Remove the foil and bake for a further 20 minutes. Allow to cool before peeling.

Meanwhile, cook the new potatoes until they are soft. Drain and cool. Put the herring in a large bowl and grate in the apple. Finely chop the potatoes and add them to the fish with the horseradish, yoghurt, crème fraîche, lemon juice and chives and season to taste. Set aside in the fridge until needed.

Whisk together the olive oil, vinegar, shallots, parsley and tarragon. Place a 7.5cm (3in) ring in the centre of a plate and spoon in the herring mixture. Carefully remove the ring. Cut the beets in half and very finely slice them. Set these around the fish salad, overlapping each slice. Top the herring with some herb leaves and spoon a little of the dressing over the top and intermittently to the far rim of the plate. Sprinkle with a little salt and pepper and serve at room temperature.

Twice-baked Roquefort soufflés

SERVES 6

1½ oz butter, plus extra for greasing

250ml (8fl oz) milk

1 onion, sliced

1 bay leaf

freshly grated nutmeg, to taste

6 whole black peppercorns

3 tbsp plain flour

salt and freshly ground black pepper

4 large eggs

175g (6oz) Roquefort, crumbled

150ml (5fl oz) double cream

small bunch of fresh chives

large bag of leaf salad, lightly dressed with good-quality oil and vinegar

I learnt to bake soufflé when, at the age of nineteen, I spent the summer cooking for a French lady in the Loire. She ordered a soufflé for lunch every day until I had created the perfect dish.

Even the most confident cooks find the idea of baking a soufflé rather intimidating, as this dish usually has to be cooked at the last minute and has a reputation for being difficult to get right. However, this recipe takes away that angst; this soufflé can be made days ahead (and even frozen) ready to be reheated for the perfect Sunday night supper or light lunch. Serve it simply with a leaf salad tossed in a light lemon vinaigrette.

Butter 6 ramekins well and set aside. Heat the milk to simmering point in a heavy-based pan along with the onion, bay leaf, nutmeg and peppercorns for 3 minutes or until warm. Remove from the heat and strain through a sieve into a jug, discarding the flavourings.

Rinse out the saucepan and gently melt the butter. Add the flour and stir with a wooden spoon for 3 minutes until the roux is glossy and pale in colour. Gradually add the warm milk, stirring continually until the sauce is thick and leaves the sides of the pan. Season with salt and pepper. Continue to cook on the lowest heat for 2 more minutes.

Remove the pan from the heat and cool slightly. Separate the eggs; put the whites into a large, clean, dry bowl and the yolks into a teacup. Add the yolks to the roux one at a time, then whisk in one-third of the Roquefort. Don't worry if the odd lump remains.

Preheat the oven to 180°C/350°F/Gas 4 and boil a full kettle. Using an electric whisk, beat the egg whites until the soft peak stage. Fold the egg whites into the roux using a folding movement to keep it light.

Divide the mixture equally between the ramekins until they are each three-quarters full. Place the ramekins in a roasting tin and pour in boiling water until it reaches halfway up the sides of the dishes. Set them in the centre of the oven and bake for 20 minutes until risen and just golden on top. Do not be tempted to open the oven door while they cook! Remove from the oven and carefully lift the ramekins from the tin to a cooling rack to prevent them cooking any further. (They will sink slightly but will expand again on their second cooking. Do not be dismayed!)

When they are completely cool, run a small palette knife around the edge and carefully turn out the soufflés onto the palm of your hand. Put them on a baking tray lined with foil. Scatter the remaining Roquefort over the top of each soufflé. They can now be stored for 24 hours in the fridge or frozen, wrapped individually in cling film.

When you are ready to serve the soufflés, preheat the oven to 180°C/350°F/Gas 4 and remove them from the fridge to allow them to return to room temperature. Butter a solid baking tray and set the soufflés on it, with a little cream poured over the top of each. Place in the centre of the oven for 15 minutes until they are well risen and golden brown.

Garnish each with some fresh chive stalks and serve them warm over a herb leaf salad.

Salad of poached pears, walnuts and Gorgonzola

This salad presents a perfect display of colours and flavours using a timeless combination of sweetened poached pears and sharp blue creamy cheese. A delicious light dish for autumn and winter.

SERVES 6

200ml (7fl oz) red wine

2 bay leaves

sprig of thyme

2 juniper berries, lightly crushed

50g (2oz) sugar

2 firm pears, ideally Conference or Comice

200g (7oz) good Gorgonzola

large bag of mixed herb salad leaves

3 tbsp Roasted red onions (page 156)

100g (3½oz) walnuts, roughly chopped

1 tbsp chopped curly parsley

Dressing

1 tbsp Dijon mustard

2 tbsp red wine vinegar

100ml (3½fl oz) walnut oil

100ml (3½fl oz) olive oil

salt and freshly ground black pepper

Pour the red wine into a small saucepan with the herbs, juniper berries and sugar and simmer for 5 minutes. Peel, quarter and core the pears and add them to the pan. Poach, uncovered, for 15 minutes, turning them every 5 minutes. (Their colour will intensify as the liquid cools.)

Meanwhile, slice the Gorgonzola into long fine slices and set aside.

Mix all the dressing ingredients in a jar and shake well to combine.

Lightly toss the salad leaves in a bowl with a little of the dressing. Arrange the leaves on the centre of a plate with the cooled pears, Gorgonzola and roasted red onions on top. Spoon a little extra dressing over each plate (although do not over-dress the leaves) and sprinkle with the walnuts and chopped parsley. Serve at once.

Seared deep-water scallops with roasted pancetta and lemon-zested risotto

This is not only a beautiful risotto, with its rainbow of colours and delicate sheen of lemon-infused oil, but the subtle flavours also balance each other perfectly. This dish calls for the best source of fresh scallops you can buy – large and tender. Take care not to overcook them as they will shrink and lose their precious juices.

This is one recipe that is particularly easy to make after a day on the beach, and one that is popular when I am visiting Martha's Vineyard, which has an abundance of deep water scallops. The risotto can be prepared in the morning up to the point of adding the stock, then finished off 30 minutes before serving.

SERVES 6

1 tbsp olive oil

30g (1oz) butter

4 shallots, peeled and finely chopped

2 lemongrass sticks,
outer leaves removed and
soft white centre finely sliced

450g (1lb) risotto rice
(carnaroli or Arborio)

150ml (5fl oz) white wine

1.5 litres (2¾ pints) vegetable stock
(you may not need it all)

18 slices fine pancetta

18 large deep-water scallops

salt and freshly ground black pepper

2 tbsp finely chopped parsley

125g (4oz) finely grated Parmesan

½ preserved lemon, finely chopped

150ml (5fl oz) Lemon oil (page 149),
to serve

Heat the oil and butter in a large heavy-based skillet and sauté the shallots and lemongrass until they are transparent. Add the rice and cook for a further 2 minutes. Pour in the white wine and simmer until the liquid has almost evaporated.

Start to ladle in enough stock to just cover the rice, then simmer at a rolling pace until the liquid is almost absorbed. Continue to add the stock in the same way, stirring gently to free any sticky grains from the base of the pan. Don't try to rush it, as time is of the essence for a really successful risotto – the cooking will take about 20 minutes.

Put the pancetta in a frying pan and sauté until very crispy. Set aside. Season the scallops and place them on some kitchen paper to dry out.

Add the parsley, Parmesan and preserved lemon once the risotto has reached a creamy point and the grains still retain some 'bite'. Check the seasoning and let the risotto stand for 5 minutes, covered with a lid.

Reheat the pancetta in a pan over a high heat, ensuring there is still just enough oil from the pancetta, then sauté the seasoned scallops for 1 minute on each side.

Divide the risotto among warm plates and set the crispy pancetta and sautéed scallops on top. Drizzle with lemon oil and serve immediately.

Smoked haddock and baked quails' egg ramekins

This recipe is my adaptation of what we used to eat on cold Sunday nights as children. It is so simple to put together; it can be assembled in the morning and left to chill in the fridge until needed, then simply baked for 15 minutes. Deliciously comforting served with warm Melba toast or good wholemeal toast.

SERVES 6

40g (1½oz) butter, cut into small cubes and chilled, plus extra for greasing

350g (12oz) undyed smoked haddock, skinned

freshly ground black pepper

60ml (2fl oz) milk

200ml (7fl oz) crème fraîche

18 quails' eggs

few sprigs of chervil or fresh chives, to serve

Preheat the oven to 190°C/375°F/Gas 5 and butter 6 ramekin dishes well. Cut the haddock into strips and discard any bones. Divide the strips equally among the ramekins and season with black pepper.

Combine the milk and crème fraîche and spread two-thirds of this mixture over the haddock. Carefully crack 3 quails' eggs into each ramekin so they are evenly spaced. Season lightly and top with the remaining crème fraîche mix. Dot with the chilled butter, set the ramekins into a roasting dish and pour in boiling water until it reaches one-third of the way up the sides of the ramekins. Bake for 15 minutes until the eggs are just set and the mixture is bubbling.

Serve with a few sprigs of chervil or chopped chives for colour.

Smoked trout, braised green lentils with asparagus and watercress

SERVES 8

500g (1lb 2oz) Puy lentils

1 carrot, peeled and quartered

2 garlic cloves, peeled

3 sprigs of thyme

2 bay leaves

200ml (7fl oz) red wine

2 tbsp red wine vinegar

1 tbsp soy sauce

200ml (7fl oz) extra virgin olive oil

1 tbsp dried cranberries

juice of 1 lemon

400g (14oz) asparagus

1 large orange

250g (9oz) watercress

50g (2oz) Italian parsley

salt and ground black pepper

8 smoked trout fillets

I first ate something similar to this at my favourite people-watching café in NoLita (North of Little Italy) in New York. Café Gitanes, on Mott and Prince Street, is always teeming with beautiful people both day and night, and their Moroccan-based food and coffee are sensational.

If you prefer you can replace the smoked trout with salmon that has been lightly smoked. The salad can be kept in the fridge for a day or two, and fresh watercress or young spinach leaves could be tossed in before serving.

Rinse the lentils under cold running water and set them in a heavy-based pan with the vegetables, red wine and enough cold water to cover the lentils completely. Bring to the boil, then lower the heat and simmer for about 25 minutes, until the lentils are well cooked but still have some bite. Drain, (discarding the liquid) and remove the carrot chunks, garlic and thyme stalks, then tip the lentils into a bowl. While they are still warm, add the red wine vinegar, soy sauce, olive oil, cranberries and lemon juice and set aside to allow the flavours to infuse. Leave to cool to room temperature.

Trim and peel the asparagus spears and set them in a pan of boiling water for 2 minutes. Remove them from the pan and run them under cold water. Drain well.

Cut away the rind and pith from the orange, then slide the knife down one side of each segment, cutting it away from the skin. Cut down the other side and pull out the segment, then toss these into the lentils with the watercress and torn parsley, and salt and pepper to taste. Spoon onto a dish, arrange the asparagus spears and trout fillets over the top and serve.

Thai beef salad

Extremely good and extremely popular, this filling, colourful, fragrant salad is so easy. Everything can be prepared in the morning, so all you need to do is dress it just before serving.

SERVES 8

4 x 225g (8oz) thick sirloin steaks

salt and freshly ground black pepper

1 tbsp vegetable oil

2 lemongrass stalks

6 large ripe limes

2 red onions, finely diced

½ tbsp olive oil

1 cucumber, peeled and shredded

4 tbsp fish sauce (nam pla)

4 red chillies, seeded and finely sliced

30 large mint leaves, sliced

4 spring onions, finely sliced

2 large bags of herb leaf salad

1 large bunch coriander, washed and roughly chopped

Season the steaks and rub with the oil. Fry the steaks until medium rare (about 3 minutes each side over a high heat), set aside for 10 minutes, then slice thinly across the grain on a diagonal.

Smash the lemongrass with the flat side of a knife, then remove the woody outer layers until you are left with the finer white part only, finely slice.

Microwave the limes for 6 seconds and squeeze their juice (if you don't have a microwave, roll the limes on a work surface with your palm until you can feel the rind warm up and loosen).

Heat a little olive oil in a pan and fry the lemongrass and onions for 3 minutes. Transfer to a large shallow bowl and add all the remaining ingredients, except the coriander. Check the seasoning. Toss in the salad leaves and arrange over a large platter or divide among individual plates. Arrange the beef strips on top of the salad, garnish with the coriander and serve.

Pecorino, asparagus and herb salad with lemon-infused oil

This is such a beautiful combination of colours and sweet flavours that it is perfect with anything. You can substitute the pecorino with feta, if you wish.

SERVES 8

500g (1lb 2oz) fresh or frozen soya, lima or baby broad beans

1 bunch of asparagus, ends trimmed

300g (10oz) petit pois

salt and freshly ground black pepper

8 tbsp Lemon oil (page 149)

handful of basil leaves

handful of mint leaves

handful of rocket leaves

1 x 400g tin artichoke hearts, cut in half and well drained

200g (7oz) young pecorino, cut into thin slices

60g (2oz) Roasted red onions (page 156)

100g (3½oz) aged Parmesan, shaved with a potato peeler

1 large lemon

Set a large pot of well-salted water to boil with a lid on. Once the water is rapidly boiling, drop in the beans and cook for 1 minute. Carefully lift them out of the water with a large slotted spoon and transfer to a colander, rinse under cold water, drain well and peel off any tough skins. Repeat this process with the asparagus and finally the peas. Toss the drained vegetables in a bowl with half the lemon oil.

Mix the herb and rocket leaves with the artichoke hearts in a separate bowl and toss lightly with salt and pepper and remaining lemon oil.

To serve, pile the leaves onto a large plate and arrange the pecorino, beans, peas and asparagus amongst the leaves. Spoon the roasted onion over the top and scatter with Parmesan shavings. Finely zest the lemon and finish with a squeeze of juice from half the lemon. Serve.

Seared tuna with pak choi salad

This stir-fry salad is simply delicious. As with all stir-fries, the time spent is in the preparation, and the dish itself should be cooked at the last minute. The fish in the recipe, however, is best prepared the day before and wrapped tightly in cling film and refrigerated. If you wish you could substitute the tuna with giant tiger prawns. Serve simply with steamed Thai rice.

SERVES 6

zest of 4 lemons

2 small red chillies, chopped

2 garlic cloves, chopped

2 large bunches of coriander, chopped

900g (2lb) very fresh, whole, sushi-grade tuna fillet

2 tsp Thai fish sauce

50g (2oz) nigella seeds

1 tbsp toasted sesame oil

2 tbsp sunflower oil

1½ tbsp very fine strips of peeled fresh ginger

6 spring onions, trimmed and sliced diagonally

2 red peppers, quartered, deseeded and finely sliced

1 tbsp tamarind paste mixed with 125ml (4fl oz) water

3 tbsp light brown soft sugar

1 tbsp lime juice

2 tbsp Thai fish sauce

300g (10oz) pak choi, roughly sliced

1 bunch of coriander, roughly chopped, plus extra to serve

Pulse the lemon zest, chillies, garlic and coriander to a paste in the blender, then coat the tuna with it. Pour over the Thai fish sauce and leave to marinate for 1 hour.

Roll the fish in the nigella seeds to coat on all sides. Heat the sesame and half the sunflower oil in a wok over a fairly high heat. Sear the tuna on all sides for 20 seconds, then set aside to rest until cool. Wrap tightly in cling film and refrigerate overnight.

When ready to serve, bring the tuna to room temperature before slicing it thinly.

Heat the remaining sunflower oil in a wok over a high flame, then add the ginger, spring onions, red peppers, tamarind paste, sugar, lime juice, fish sauce and the pak choi. Bring to the boil quickly, tossing the ingredients well, and remove to a large platter. Lay the sliced tuna over this warm salad and serve with the coriander scattered over.

Asparagus, dill and prawn salad

May is the month for asparagus. This colourful salad is perfect both for lunch or a light supper and makes the most of our glorious English asparagus during its short season.

SERVES 8

3 bunches asparagus, washed well and cut in half or thirds

250g (9oz) baby broad beans

250g (9oz) sliced smoked salmon, cut into thick strips

675g (1½lb) cooked large tiger prawns, drained

½ cucumber, peeled, seeded and cut into sticks

6 tbsp olive oil

juice of 1 lemon

large bunch of dill, finely chopped

sea salt and freshly ground black pepper

400g (14oz) rocket or watercress

1 loaf olive ciabatta or herb foccacia, warmed

Blanch the asparagus for 3 minutes in well-salted boiling water. Using a large slotted spoon, remove the spears and plunge them into a bowl of iced water, to keep their vibrant colour. Set aside to drain. Repeat the blanching process with the broad beans for 2 minutes. Transfer to a colander, place under cold running water, then set aside to drain and cool completely.

In a large bowl, combine the asparagus, beans, salmon, prawns and cucumber. In a large jam jar, mix the oil, lemon, dill and seasoning. Shake until the ingredients are well blended.

Dress the salad at the last minute and toss in the rocket. Serve with lots of warm, crusty herb breads.

Two stuffed chooks

Roast chicken is always a crowd pleaser, and this easy and delicious dish is perfect for an English summer, as it can be cooked on the barbecue or in the oven. Removing the backbone and flattening out the chicken gives it a shorter cooking time and allows the stuffing to retain its flavours. Always buy the best cornfed free-range chicken you can afford as it tastes quite different.

For a more wintry version, try the mushroom stuffing recipe opposite and serve with a creamy Parmesan-flavoured mash.

SERVES 6

Herb and ricotta stuffing

500g (1lb 2oz) ricotta cheese

mixed bunch of chervil, flatleaf parsley and chives, chopped

zest and juice of 2 lemons

salt and freshly ground black pepper

1 medium cornfed chicken

1 lemon, sliced

olive oil

few sprigs of thyme

Preheat the oven to 200°C/400°F/Gas 6. Mix the ricotta, herbs, lemon zest and juice and salt and pepper together.

Cut the chicken down the backbone with a sharp heavy knife. Turn the chicken over onto the breast side and, using the palm of your hand, flatten the chicken. Loosen the skin from the meat using your hand to create a pocket all the way down into the legs. Stuff the ricotta mixture under the skin to fill the pocket and gently pummel the mixture so that it is evenly spread under the skin, taking care not to break the skin.

Lay the lemon slices over the base of a roasting tin and set the chicken skin-side on top. Cover with little oil, salt and whole thyme sprigs. Bake in the oven for 50 minutes, until golden and the juices run clear when the thigh joint is pierced. Alternatively, place it on some thick foil and cook over a hot barbecue for 25 minutes on each side until it is totally cooked through. In both cases, leave to rest for 10 minutes, covered, before serving in thick slices.

Mushroom, thyme and lemon zest stuffing

olive oil, for cooking

250g (9oz) chestnut mushrooms, halved

180g (6oz) lardons

zest and juice of 1 large lemon

1 bunch of thyme, leaves removed

250g (9oz) mascarpone

4 shallots, finely sliced

3 garlic cloves, peeled and cut in half

300g (10oz) mixed mushrooms, such as portobello, oyster

salt and freshly ground black pepper

30 sage leaves

olive oil, for frying

200ml (7fl oz) single cream

white truffle oil

Heat some oil in a frying pan and sauté the chestnut mushrooms and lardons until crispy. Leave to cool, then transfer to a food processor with the lemon zest and juice, thyme leaves, salt and pepper and 1 large tablespoon of mascarpone. Stuff the chicken as described opposite.

Layer the shallots, garlic and mushrooms over the base of an ovenproof dish and place the chicken on top. Cover with a little oil and seasoning and cook as opposite.

Towards the end of the cooking time, fry the sage leaves briefly in a little oil until crisp but not coloured. Set aside on some kitchen paper. Remove the chicken from the pan and set aside to rest, covered in foil. Stir in the remaining mascarpone and cream into the chicken juices and heat through. Carve the chicken, very lightly drizzle the slices with a little truffle oil and scatter with the crispy sage leaves. Serve with the creamy sauce alongside.

Lamb stuffed with couscous, feta and spinach

This joint is a little fiddly to tie, so often I ask my friendly butcher to do it for me once I've stuffed it. I like to serve this at room temperature, which allows the meat to rest and hold its shape, and gives the lamb a more pronounced flavour. It is excellent served cold too.

SERVES 8

125g (4oz) Israeli couscous

2kg (4½lb) boned lamb

olive oil, for cooking

2 shallots, diced

180g (6oz) Greek feta

250g (9oz) frozen chopped spinach, defrosted and well drained

4 ripe tomatoes, chopped

2 garlic cloves, finely chopped

1 medium bunch of mint and parsley

zest of 1 lemon, juice of 2

salt and freshly ground black pepper

Put the couscous in a large bowl and pour enough boiling water over it to just cover. Set aside for 10 minutes to allow the grains to absorb the liquid. Fork through the mixture to separate the grains.

Preheat the oven to 180°C/350°F/Gas 4. Trim the lamb of any excess fat and lay the piece flat on a work surface.

Heat 1 tablespoon of olive oil in a frying pan and sauté the shallots until transparent. Add to the couscous along with the feta, spinach, tomatoes, garlic, herbs, lemon and seasoning. Stir well to combine all the ingredients, then spread this over the meat and roll it up as tightly as possible. Tie the string every few inches along the roll. Season, then rub with a little oil and some lemon juice and cook in the oven for 1 hour, basting the meat with its juices three times during cooking.

Allow the meat to rest for 10 minutes, covered with foil, before carving it into thick slices.

Pork, veal and chicken terrine

In this recipe, pork, veal and chicken balance each other perfectly, and the cranberry and port sauce makes a fruity and pretty accompaniment. All terrines are best served after 24 hours in the fridge and should be sliced when chilled and served at room temperature. This dish will keep for up to a week in the fridge.

SERVES 8

3 fresh bay leaves

250g (9oz) streaky bacon

250g (9oz) veal mince

125g (4½oz) pork mince

125g (4½oz) chicken mince

2 large onions, minced

2 garlic cloves

125g (4½oz) pistachio nuts

4 juniper berries

1 egg

1 tbsp green peppercorns in brine, drained

2 tbsp brandy

1 tsp dried basil

1 tsp chopped sage

1 tbsp chopped parsley

salt and freshly ground black pepper

For the sauce

115g (4oz) port

115g (4oz) cranberry sauce

zest and juice of 1 small lemon and 1 large orange

Place the bay leaves in the base of a loaf tin and line the tin loosely with the bacon, reserving enough to cover the top of the terrine.

Mix together the minced meats with the minced onions. Whiz the garlic, pistachio nuts and juniper berries roughly in a blender. Add to the meats along with the egg, peppercorns, brandy, basil, sage, parsley, salt and pepper. Mix together until well combined.

Preheat the oven to 180°C/350°F/Gas 4. Pack the mixture tightly into the loaf tin and lay the remaining bacon over the top. Cover with foil, place in a roasting tin filled with enough boiling water to reach halfway up the sides of the loaf tin, and bake for 1½ hours. Cool, then leave in the fridge overnight to set.

Make the sauce simply by combining the port, cranberry sauce and citrus zest and juice. Bring to the boil, then lower the heat and simmer for about 15 minutes until the sauce is reduced by half. Allow to cool before serving alongside the terrine.

Carrot cake

SERVES 8

300g (10oz) carrots, peeled and roughly chopped

1 piece stem ginger in syrup, reserve 1 tbsp of the syrup

225g (8oz) unsalted butter, softened

225g (8oz) light brown muscovado sugar

grated zest of 1 orange

4 eggs, beaten

250g (9oz) self-raising flour

2 tsp baking powder

½ tsp ground cinnamon

50g (2oz) ground almonds

85g (3oz) walnuts, roughly chopped

For the icing

350g (12oz) cream cheese

50g (2oz) icing sugar

2 tbsp fresh orange juice

Stem ginger and orange zest add a zingy twist to this delicious easy-to-make cake. It's a real favourite in our family for afternoon tea or as a dessert. It freezes perfectly too.

Preheat the oven to 180°C/350°F/Gas 4. Lightly grease a 20cm (8in) round, deep cake tin and line it with baking parchment.

Place the carrots, stem ginger, syrup and 1 tablespoon of cold water in a food processor and blend until the mixture becomes a pulp. Empty the mixture into a clean bowl.

Using the same food processor bowl, blend the butter, sugar and orange zest until pale and thick. Add the eggs one at a time – if the mixture curdles slightly, do not despair, just add a spoonful of flour. Then add the flour, baking powder and cinnamon and pulse everything on a low speed until just combined. Add the almonds, half the walnuts and the carrot pulp. Pulse again until just combined.

Spoon the mixture into the prepared tin, level the surface and bake for about 1 hour until it is risen and is golden on top. Insert a skewer into the centre to test the cake – if it comes out clean it is cooked. Carefully remove the cake to a wire rack to cool completely.

In a food processor or using a hand-held blender, blend the cream cheese, icing sugar and orange juice until smooth. Spread the icing over the cooled cake, sprinkle with the remaining chopped walnuts and serve.

Chocolate fruit and nut block

This extremely rich block will keep for up to a month, wrapped in foil, in the fridge and is wonderfully popular as an all-important sweet fix to finish a meal and break all those good diet resolutions! It is also very quick and easy to put together.

SERVES 12

500g (1lb 2oz) plain chocolate

120g (4½oz) shelled pistachio nuts

120g (4½oz) Brazil nuts, coarsely chopped

120g (4½oz) pecan nuts, coarsely chopped

120g (4½oz) glacé cherries

120g (4½oz) raisins

400g (14oz) condensed milk

1 tbsp brandy

Break the chocolate into a microwaveable bowl and cook on High for 4 minutes, or in a heatproof bowl set over a pan of simmering water. Stir in the remaining ingredients, adding the brandy last.

Line a loaf tin with foil and spread the chocolate mix evenly into the tin. Cover and refrigerate for at least 3 hours before turning it out of its tin onto a board. Slice into thick pieces, then into bite-sized squares.

Tarte Tatin

This is a classic pudding that I am asked to serve time and time again. Having experimented with a variety of apples, I think it works best with Granny Smiths; they can be slightly tart and hold their shape well. This pudding improves in flavour if left for a day before serving, and it freezes perfectly. Serve slightly warmed with crème fraîche, Orange mascarpone cream (see page 157) or good vanilla ice cream.

SERVES 8

70g (2½oz) unsalted butter

250g (9oz) refined golden granulated sugar

6–7 Granny Smiths apples, peeled, cored and cut into quarters

1 x 500g pack puff pastry, at room temperature

flour, for dusting

Preheat the oven to 200°C/400°F/Gas 6. Melt the butter and sugar in a medium-sized, heavy-based frying pan that has an ovenproof handle, gently at first, then increasing the heat until the mixture turns a toffee colour. At this point, carefully place the apple quarters very tightly around the outside of the frying pan, working towards the centre until the pan is packed full. Take extra care not to touch the burning caramel and keep the apples very tightly packed. Turn off the heat.

Roll out the pastry on a cool, floured surface and cut to form a roughly round shape just larger than the size of the pan. Carefully drape the pastry over the apples, tucking the corners underneath the outside apples. Place in the centre of the oven for 30 minutes until the pastry is risen and golden.

Remove, leave to cool slightly, and then, very carefully and using good oven gloves or dry tea towels, turn the pan upside down over a larger round plate with a slight rim. Should any of the caramel remain stuck to the bottom of the pan, gently reheat the pan until the mixture is runny and able to be poured over the apples. Allow to cool a little, then serve.

Hazelnut meringue with raspberries

SERVES 8

150g (5oz) hazelnuts

4 egg whites, at room temperature

pinch of salt

200g (7oz) refined golden caster sugar

½ tsp white vinegar

300ml (½ pint) whipping cream

750g (1½lb) raspberries

16 cape gooseberries

fresh mint leaves, to serve

This is possibly one of the all-time great desserts; it has never worn with the food trends and it is still very popular today. The teaspoon of vinegar is the trick to keeping it light, like a pavlova. The meringue can be made a week in advance and stored in an airtight container.

Toast the hazelnuts in a dry frying pan until golden. Allow to cool, then grind in a blender until they are like coarse sand.

Whisk the egg whites in a clean dry bowl with the salt until stiff. Whisk in 1 tablespoon of sugar every 2 or 3 minutes until it is all mixed in. Fold in the vinegar and ground nuts.

Preheat the oven to 150°C/300°F/Gas 2. Cover two baking sheets with baking paper cut into 25cm (10in) diameter circles and divide the meringue mixture equally between the two.

Bake in the oven for 1¼ hours, then turn off the oven and leave the meringue inside to cool. When completely cool, remove and carefully peel the paper off the base of each meringue. Store them carefully in an airtight container or freeze until needed.

When ready to serve, whip the cream and spread half of it on one meringue. Top with the raspberries and the second meringue. Spread the remaining cream over the top of this meringue and pile over the remaining raspberries and the cape gooseberries and add the mint leaves for decoration. Chill in the fridge until needed.

Food for Friends & Family

"I love cooking on a grand scale – putting all the details in place for the food itself and also on the table to create a really good-looking party – but sometimes an event calls for something more informal. Buffet food has its place to serve large numbers of people, but frankly this can in fact end up being an awful lot of work.

Fork food is a fantastic compromise between a seated dinner and a buffet, and better still it offers the opportunity to entertain and feed lots of people with minimal effort! This sort of food is simplicity itself, served in warm bowls as one-pot wonders for a large party of friends, it is fuss-free and requires minimal cutlery – just a fork will do.

Many of the recipes I've included here are well known, almost old-fashioned, but each has a contemporary twist. Once again, all recipes can be prepared well ahead and finished off effortlessly at the last moment, leaving you free to mix with mates and chat between mouthfuls."

Smoked kipper gratins

Kippers, like anchovies, have a huge amount of flavour, are cheap and, to my mind, are much underused – if you can lay your hands on some Arbroath smokies, even more of a treat awaits you. You don't have to use kippers here, any smoked fish works well. This recipe is not only simple but also very quick to make and can be prepared up to a day ahead and kept in the fridge to be baked when needed. Serve with good, warm, wholegrain toast.

SERVES 8

4 smoked kippers

400ml (14fl oz) double cream

1 tbsp grain mustard

8 firm ripe plum tomatoes, peeled and deseeded

8 basil leaves or
1 tsp finely chopped parsley

freshly ground black pepper

115g (4oz) grated strong Cheddar

50g (2oz) grated Parmesan

Peel the skin off the kippers and cut the fish into strips, removing any larger bones. Divide half the kippers between 8 ramekins or 1 large ovenproof dish and spread them out to cover the bases.

Mix the cream with the mustard until well combined. Layer the tomatoes and basil or parsley over the fish, topping with half of the mustard cream. Add the rest of the fish, a grinding of pepper and the remaining cream. Scatter over the cheeses and set the dishes in the fridge for an hour or until needed.

Preheat the oven to 180°C/350°F/Gas 4 and, when ready, position the gratins on the top shelf and bake for about 20 minutes, until they are bubbling and golden brown. Serve immediately.

Salmon and prawn kedgeree

This is not the traditional version of this classic British-Empire dish, as my recipe does not have so much as a hint of curry powder. However, it is just as delicious and is ever-popular for informal suppers or brunch.

SERVES 6

660g (1½lb) firm white fish, such as haddock, turbot or brill

450g (1lb) salmon fillet

juice of 1½ lemons

salt and freshly ground black pepper

115g (4oz) butter

3 eggs

generous pinch of saffron strands

270g (10oz) basmati rice

250ml (8fl oz) single cream

large bunch of flatleaf parsley, roughly chopped

1½ tsp cayenne pepper

200g (7oz) large prawns, cooked, peeled and drained

Most of this kedgeree can be prepared ahead, only the rice needs to be cooked just before serving. The other ingredients can be stirred into the rice and left for 10 minutes for the flavours to infuse, then heated and served piping hot. Be careful when adding the cayenne pepper – you just want a little for a bit of a kick.

Put the fish in a microwaveable dish with half the lemon juice, and season with salt and pepper. Dot the fish with a large knob of the butter, cover with a plate and microwave on Medium (600 watts) for 6 minutes. Remove from the microwave and, leaving the dish covered, allow the fish to steam and cool. Flake the fish, removing any skin and bones.

Melt a large knob of butter in a small non-stick frying pan over a medium heat. Season the eggs, beat them gently, then pour half into the pan and cook as an omelette. Repeat with the rest of the egg. Roughly slice both omelettes into strips.

Mix the saffron strands in a small bowl with 1 tablespoon of boiling water, using the spoon to crush through the strands to release their colour and flavour. Heat a large knob of butter in a large heavy-based saucepan, add the rice and fry for 2 minutes. Add the saffron and its water with a further 375ml (12oz) cold water. Cover and bring to the boil. Reduce the heat and simmer for 15 minutes or until the rice is just tender.

Melt the rest of the butter in a small pan with the cream, remaining lemon juice, parsley, cayenne and salt and pepper.

Carefully fold the fish and omelette into the rice, taking care not to break them up. Mix in the prawns and cream sauce and check the seasoning. Turn off the heat and leave the kedgeree to rest for 8 minutes, covered. Serve on warm plates.

Mussels with saffron, fennel and spinach

A perfect winter warmer when mussels are in season and at their freshest. Serve with warm crusty white bread and good French unsalted butter.

SERVES 4

1kg (2¼lb) fresh mussels

100ml (3½fl oz) dry white wine

80ml (3fl oz) Pernod

3 shallots, peeled and finely chopped

4 bay leaves

fresh thyme sprigs

10 black peppercorns

50g (2oz) unsalted butter

1 medium fennel bulb, finely sliced

2 tsp saffron strands

salt and freshly ground black pepper

4 tbsp water

250ml (8fl oz) crème fraîche

150g (5½oz) baby spinach leaves, well washed

Clean the mussels well under cold running water, scrubbing any grit off the shells. Remove the tenacious beards and discard any opened shells or those that float in a sink full of cold water.

Pour the white wine and Pernod into a heavy-based pan with the shallots, bay leaves, thyme and peppercorns and bring to a simmer. Add the mussels, cover the pan and increase the heat to a gentle boil. Cook for 4–5 minutes, shaking the pan occasionally to encourage the mussels to open. Tip the cooked mussels into a colander set over a bowl and reserve the cooking liquid. Pick through the mussels and discard any that are unopened, along with the bay leaves, thyme and peppercorns.

Wipe the pan clean, return it to the heat and add the butter. Once it has melted, add the fennel, saffron and a little salt and pepper. Cover the pan and sweat the onions over a gentle heat for 10 minutes.

Return the mussels to the pan along with the water, crème fraîche and wine/Pernod reduction. Stir well and simmer for 2 minutes, then add the spinach, stir, cover the pan and cook briefly until wilted. Serve immediately in warmed bowls.

Fish pie

Everyone has their own favourite fish pie recipe – this is mine. I like to use three different types of fish here, for their taste, texture and colour, but choose your favourites if you prefer particular fish for their cost, flavour or availability.

SERVES 10

1 x large fillet (approx. 400g/14oz) chunky white fish (haddock or cod)

1 x medium fillet (250g/9oz) salmon

1 x large fillet (approx. 400g/14oz) undyed smoked fish (haddock or cod)

1 large onion, sliced

1 bay leaf

salt and freshly ground black pepper

splash of milk

300ml (10fl oz) white wine

160g (5½oz) butter

2–3 tbsp plain flour

juice and zest of ½ lemon

250g (9oz) large peeled prawns, drained

large bunch parsley, finely chopped

24 quails' eggs, cooked (4 minutes) and peeled

mashed potato made from 8 large red waxed potatoes

125g (4oz) Gran padano, grated

Put the fish fillets, half the onion, the bay leaf, salt and pepper, milk and white wine in a heavy-based saucepan over a medium heat. Simmer gently, covered, for 10 minutes then leave to cool completely with the lid on.

Carefully remove the fish from the pan using a slotted spoon and transfer to a plate. Strain the cooking liquid through a sieve into a jug and set aside. Carefully skin the cooked fish and remove any large bones, break the fillets into large chunks and set aside.

Heat the butter in the same saucepan over a medium heat and fry the remaining onion until golden. Add the flour and cook, stirring, for 1 minute. Slowly pour the strained fish cooking liquid into the pan, stirring constantly to make a smooth sauce. Add more milk if necessary, then add the lemon juice and zest and stir until you have a thick white sauce. Remove from the heat and carefully fold in the prawns, fish and parsley. Check the seasoning and gently spoon the mixture into a shallow ovenproof dish.

Preheat the oven to 200°C/400°F/Gas 6. Dot the quails' eggs evenly over the fish, cover everything with the mashed potato and scatter over the grated cheese. Bake in the oven for 30 minutes until piping hot and golden on top.

Thai-style marinated monkfish and salmon

Monkfish, though fairly expensive, has a lovely meaty texture and holds its shape well when cooked, so it is perfect for stuffing into the salmon fillet in this recipe. This dish is extremely quick to make and is perfect for preparing the day before. It never fails to impress, with its beautiful colours and delicately spiced Thai flavours.

Lemon-zested rice with fresh coriander is a perfect accompaniment to this light dish, and perhaps some fine French beans that have been just cooked so they still retain some crunch.

Heat the butter in a large frying pan until foaming. Season the monkfish and sauté in the hot butter for 4 minutes on all sides. Trim the salmon into a thick rectangle and carefully slice a pocket lengthways through the centre of the salmon. Push the monkfish into the pocket.

Mix all the marinade ingredients together and pour into a lidded container. Add the fish, turning it in the marinade to cover it on all sides, then seal the container and transfer it to the fridge to marinate overnight.

Preheat the oven to 180°C/350°F/Gas 4. Tip the fish, with its marinade, into a baking dish lined with foil and cook, uncovered, for 15 minutes, basting regularly. Finish it off under the grill for a few minutes until cooked through.

Set aside to cool slightly before slicing into 8 pieces and serving with a little of its cooking juices.

SERVES 8

40g (1½oz) butter

whole monkfish fillet (enough for 7 people)

salt and freshly ground black pepper

1 side of salmon, filleted and skinned

The marinade

2 tbsp light soy sauce

2 tbsp fish sauce

2 tsp chilli sauce

3cm (1in) piece of ginger, peeled and grated

4 garlic cloves, crushed

1 lemongrass stalk, outer leaves removed and soft white centre finely sliced

zest and juice of 2 limes

2 tsp oyster sauce

2 tsp saki or white wine

2 tsp chopped coriander

juice of 1 lemon

Thai green chicken and cashew curry

This classic recipe has been adapted by many cooks and is much loved by all, so I felt I had to include it – but with my own slight adaptations. Don't be tempted to use shop-bought curry paste, fresh is more aromatic and will keep for a week in a sealed container in the fridge. The flavour of the green sauce improves on keeping, so prepare this curry a day or two before serving.

Poach the chicken in a large pan with the carrot, bay and lime leaves, celery, whole lemongrass and enough water just to cover, with the lid on, for 20 minutes. Allow to cool in its stock. Once cooled, remove the chicken thighs and cut each one into three.

Place the green chillies, sliced lemongrass, lime zest and juice, half the coriander (with stalks), cumin seeds, garlic, shallots and ginger in a food processor and blend to a coarse paste.

Heat a wok over a hight heat, and when hot scoop the cream from the top of the coconut milk into the pan. Stir until it is boiling and begins to fry slightly and crackle. Add half the green curry paste, stir well and allow this to reduce and thicken before adding the remainder of the paste and coconut milk. Boil for 10 minutes until the sauce is slightly thickened. Add the chicken pieces and warm through. Check the seasoning and serve with the remaining coriander, roughly chopped, sliced red chilli and a little lemon zest sprinkled over.

SERVES 6

8 boned chicken thighs, skinned

1 carrot

1 bay leaf

2 Kaffir lime leaves

1 celery stick

2 lemongrass stalks, 1 whole, 1 peeled and sliced (soft white centre only)

6 green chillies

zest and juice of 6 limes

1 large bunch of coriander, washed and drained

1 tsp cumin seeds, toasted

4 garlic cloves, peeled

6 shallots, peeled and cut in half

5cm (2in) piece of fresh ginger, peeled

2 x 400ml tins coconut milk

4 tbsp fish sauce

2 tsp sugar

200g (7oz) cashews, roughly chopped

1 red chilli, deseeded and very finely sliced

zest of 1 lemon

Thai lobster chowder

The aromatics of this soup are wonderful for a streaming cold! If you can't get lobster you can use monkfish fillets or even chicken breasts instead. This simple, speedy chowder can be cooked ahead and stored for several days in the fridge.

SERVES 6

1½litres (2¾ pints) good-quality chicken stock

zest of 3 limes, juice of 2

1 Spanish onion, finely chopped

3 lemongrass stalks, outer leaves removed and soft white centre finely sliced

350g (12oz) Charlotte or red potatoes, peeled and diced

salt and freshly ground black pepper

1 tbsp sunflower oil

2 shallots, finely chopped

2 small red chillies, deseeded and finely chopped

1 large garlic clove, crushed

3 tsp grated fresh ginger

300g (10oz) shiitake mushrooms, sliced

800g (1¾lb) lobster meat

400g (14oz) large uncooked peeled prawns

1 x 400ml tin coconut milk

1 bunch of coriander, leaves and stalks roughly chopped

Pour the stock into a large pan and add the lime zest, onion, lemongrass and potatoes and some seasoning. Bring to the boil then simmer for 10 minutes, covered, until the potatoes are soft.

Heat the oil in a frying pan and sauté the shallots, chillies, garlic and ginger. Add the mushrooms and cook until lightly browned. Transfer everything to the soup.

Just before serving, add the lobster, prawns, coconut milk, lime juice and coriander to the soup. Cover with a lid and bring to a simmer, taste for seasoning and serve in warmed bowls.

Gurnard gratin

This is one of my simplest supper dishes and can be prepared in just five minutes. Gurnard is a dense, bland fish that is widely available in the Atlantic and Mediterranean regions. It is inexpensive and to my mind underused, and it perfectly complements this cheese sauce. It can be substituted for monkfish if you want a more expensive treat. If you're not a fan of fennel, use tomatoes or cucumber instead. Serve with crushed, minted new potatoes and wilted young spinach or watercress leaves to mop up the wonderful sauce.

SERVES 6

2 large fennel bulbs

300ml (10fl oz) double cream

1.1kg (2½lb) gurnard fillets, skinned and cut into 6 pieces

salt and freshly ground black pepper

50g (2oz) grated Parmesan

50g (2oz) grated Gruyère cheese

2 tbsp chopped flatleaf parsley

Remove any bruised or damaged outer fennel leaves and thickly slice the fennel bulbs horizontally, removing the triangular core from the base. Blanche the fennel in a pan of boiling salted water for 2 minutes. Drain well and arrange over the base of a large, shallow ovenproof dish.

Preheat the oven to 180°C/350°F/Gas 4. Pour a thin layer of cream over the fennel, season the fish and place over the fennel. Pour over the remaining cream. Sprinkle over the cheeses and bake in the oven for 30 minutes. Heat the grill to High and place the gratin beneath it for 5 more minutes until the top is golden brown.

Cool slightly and sprinkle over the chopped parsley before serving.

Courgette and lemon-zested ricotta cannelloni

SERVES 8

50g (2oz) butter

1 large onion, finely chopped

2 garlic cloves, finely chopped

900g (2lb) sliced courgettes

small bunch of thyme

salt and freshly ground black pepper

2 eggs, beaten

450g (1lb) ricotta cheese

175g (6oz) grated Parmesan

zest of 1 lemon

1 tbsp chopped parsley

500ml (16fl oz) good-quality fresh
tomato sauce (bought or homemade)

24 cannelloni tubes

500ml (16fl oz) crème fraîche

2 tbsp chopped tarragon

1 tsp chopped lemon thyme

Basil oil (see page 149), to serve

A delicious baked pasta that will satisfy vegetarians and meat-eaters alike. If you prefer, as a seasonal variation you could substitute the courgette for broccoli. Serve with a good leaf salad lightly dressed with a lemon vinaigrette. (For the staunch meat-eaters, it also works really well with some grilled lamb.)

Heat the butter in a large pan and cook the onion and garlic until soft. Add the courgettes, thyme, salt and pepper and a little water. Cover and cook for about 8 minutes until the courgettes are just tender. Strain through a colander, discard the thyme stalks and coarsely chop the courgettes in a food processor. Transfer to a large bowl to cool.

Once cool, add the beaten eggs, ricotta, half the Parmesan, lemon zest, parsley and seasoning to the courgettes.

Spoon the tomato sauce over the base of a large rectangular baking dish, then, using a teaspoon (this is the messy part!), spoon the mixture into the cannelloni tubes. Arrange these in a single layer in the baking dish.

Preheat the oven to 180°C/350°F/Gas 4. In a small pan, gently boil the crème fraîche until it is reduced by a third, then add the chopped tarragon and lemon thyme. Spoon this mixture over the cannelloni tubes and cover with the remaining Parmesan. Bake in the oven for about 40 minutes until it is bubbling and golden brown on top. Allow to cool for 5 minutes, then serve drizzled with basil oil.

Kidneys turbigo

This is a slightly dated, but no less popular, recipe that I fondly remember eating as a child. It is economical to make and also freezes very well. I like to prepare this dish ahead of time and toss the kidneys back in to reheat just before serving. Take care not to overcook the kidneys, though, or they will lose their tenderness. Delicious with a mix of wild and brown rice and minted petit pois.

SERVES 8

18 shallots

16 lamb or veal kidneys

125g (4½oz) butter

12 chipolata sausages

250g (9oz) chestnut mushrooms, halved

1 tbsp flour

1 tbsp tomato purée

1 tbsp grain mustard

2 tbsp sherry

240ml (8fl oz) double cream

360ml (12fl oz) beef stock

bay leaf

8 fried French bread, to serve

finely chopped parsley, to serve

Blanch the shallots in a pan of boiling salted water for 2 minutes. Tip into a colander, drain, and refresh under cold water. Set aside to drain.

Slice the kidneys in half horizontally and, using kitchen scissors, cut out and discard the white core. Melt the butter in a large frying pan and cook the kidneys in it over a high heat for about 3 minutes until browned on all sides. Set aside. Chop each chipolata into 3 and brown in the same pan. Toss in the mushrooms and drained shallots and cook until browned. Reduce the heat, then add the flour, tomato purée, mustard, sherry, cream, stock and bay leaf to the pan and bring to the boil. Cook, stirring, for 10 minutes. Return the kidneys to the pan and warm through for a few minutes.

Serve on top of the fried French bread, sprinkled with parsley.

Middle Eastern shepherd's pie

A great winter warmer with a twist, this is a delicious spiced alternative to the classic shepherd's pie. Don't be put off by the long list of ingredients, as this is actually very easy to make and freezes perfectly, so you can always make double and freeze one quantity for another day.

SERVES 6

1 large aubergine, sliced thickly

salt and freshly ground black pepper

2 tbsp olive oil

1.5kg (3lb 3 oz) minced lamb

2 onions, roughly chopped

2 celery sticks, finely chopped

2 carrots, peeled and diced

5 garlic cloves, crushed

2 tbsp Roasted mixed spices (page 148)

2 tbsp flour

300ml (10fl oz) veal stock

zest and juice of 1 orange

80g (3oz) raisins, soaked and drained

5 tbsp tomato purée

450g (1lb) potatoes, peeled and chopped

950g (2lb) parsnips, peeled and chopped

50g (2oz) butter

4 tbsp double cream

1 tsp ground cinnamon

2 tsp cayenne pepper

80g (3oz) toasted blanched whole almonds

Caramelised shallot topping (page 154), to serve

Sprinkle the aubergine slices with salt and set them in a colander for 30 minutes to draw out the liquid. Rinse briefly, pat dry with kitchen paper and cut into cubes. Heat the oil in a large pan over a high heat and brown the lamb all over. Remove the meat with a slotted spoon and transfer to a plate, then lower the heat and cook the onions, celery, carrots and aubergine until golden. Add the garlic and roasted spices and return the lamb to the pan. Add the flour and stir for a minute before adding the stock, orange zest and juice, raisins and tomato purée. Simmer for 40 minutes, stirring occasionally, until the stock reduces and you have a good thick sauce.

Boil the potatoes and parsnips in separate pans of boiling salted water until they are both soft. Drain well then mash them together. Tip them into a blender with the butter, cream and spices, and blend until smooth.

Preheat the oven to 180°C/350°F/Gas 4. Stir the almonds into the meat and spoon the mixture into an ovenproof dish. Top with the parsnip mash. Bake in the oven for 20 minutes until lightly browned on top and piping hot.

Serve topped with the caramelised shallots.

Navarin of lamb

Traditionally a navarin made the most of spring lamb and vegetables, but this version can be served throughout the year. I like to serve this with a leek and potato purée, which mops up the wonderful sweet wine sauce perfectly. If you want to prepare this ahead and freeze it, do so before you add the shallots, mangetout, turnips and carrots, then simply add these in the last 10 minutes of reheating the dish.

SERVES 6

2 tbsp good-quality olive oil

1 tbsp butter

1½ kg (3lb 3oz) boned leg lamb or neck fillet, cut into 2.5cm (1in) cubes, fat removed

salt and freshly ground black pepper, to taste

100ml (3½fl oz) brandy

60ml (2fl oz) sherry vinegar

2 tbsp cornflour

2 tbsp redcurrant jelly

2 tbsp tomato purée

200ml (7fl oz) veal or chicken stock

225ml (7½fl oz) red wine

1 medium onion, peeled and finely sliced

5 garlic cloves, crushed

3 large carrots, peeled and cut into sticks

1 tsp dried rosemary

1 tsp dried thyme

1 bay leaf

12 shallots

500g (1lb 2 oz) mangetout

12 baby carrots, washed and halved lengthways

12 baby turnips, washed and halved lengthways

50g (2oz) finely chopped parsley

Heat the oil and butter in a large heavy-based casserole over a high heat. Season the lamb and sauté the cubes in batches until browned, taking care not to overcrowd the pan. Set aside. Drain off any excess oil and return the pan to a lower heat, then add the brandy and heat it gently to deglaze the pan. Return the lamb to the pan, add the vinegar, cornflour, redcurrant jelly, tomato purée, stock and red wine. Boil for 5 minutes, stirring constantly. Add the onion, garlic, carrots, herbs and seasoning. Cover and cook over a medium heat or in an oven preheated to 160°C/325°F/Gas 3 for 1½ hours. (If freezing the casserole, do so at this point.)

Peel the shallots and wash the mangetout. Bring a medium saucepan of salted water to the boil, add the shallots and boil for about 4 minutes, until tender but firm. Remove the shallots to a colander using a large slotted spoon and rinse under cold running water to stop the cooking process. Set aside to drain. Repeat the blanching process with the mangetout for 1 minute, followed by the carrots and turnips for 2 minutes. Make sure the vegetables are well submerged. Again, hold the vegetables under cold running water immediately after blanching, and drain well. Add all the vegetables to the casserole for the last 10 minutes, along with the chopped parsley.

Season to taste and serve in large, deep warm bowls.

Baked ham with apricots and cider

A baked ham makes a perfect lunch at Christmas or any Sunday in the year. Gammon is cheap, easily available and simple to cook – and tastes so much better than processed bought ham, too. If you have any left over, freeze it in chunks or slices, or use it in a million different ways and dishes. Served hot, I like to eat ham with some good mash and a generous dollop of old-fashioned parsley sauce.

SERVES 8

2.2–2.5kg (5–5½lb) unsmoked gammon

1 carrot, cut in half

1 celery stick, cut in half

2 bay leaves

8 black peppercorns

1 x 22g jar whole cloves

2 tbsp Dijon mustard

1 tbsp unrefined dark muscovado sugar

1 tbsp runny honey

6cm (2½in) piece of root ginger, peeled, chopped and puréed

20 dried apricots

600ml (1 pint) cider

Remove any packaging and place the gammon in a large saucepan with the carrot, celery, bay leaves, peppercorns and enough cold water to cover. Bring to the boil, covered, then lower the heat and simmer for 45 minutes, removing any scum that comes to the surface with a large spoon. Leave in the pan, covered, until cool.

Once cooled, remove and trim away the outer rind without cutting through the string. With a sharp small knife, score a diamond pattern over the fat on top of the ham and then, using a long carving fork, make several holes within each diamond. Finally, stud each diamond with a whole clove. Transfer the meat to a large roasting tin.

Preheat the oven to 160°C/325°F/Gas 3. Mix the mustard, sugar, honey and ginger together and spread half this mix over the top of the ham. Scatter the apricots around the base of the ham, pour over half the cider, cover the whole tin with foil and cook in the oven for 1 hour. Baste with the glaze and juices every 20 minutes, adding more cider as needed.

Remove the foil, spread the remaining honey-mustard mixture over the ham and return to the oven, uncovered, for another 45 minutes. Transfer the ham to a serving plate and allow it rest for 10 minutes. Tip the caramelised apricot sauce from the bottom of the roasting tin into a jug and serve alongside the carved ham.

Normandy pheasant

I love winter, not least for its seasonal supply of fresh pheasant. This bird has such a wonderful game taste and makes a delicious change from chicken. Here you need a jointed bird, but don't throw away the carcass, as it will make excellent stock for the freezer. This recipe could also be made using partridge or guinea fowl. This is excellent with wintry veg such as spiced red cabbage, caramelised braised chicory and creamy mashed potatoes.

SERVES 6

100g (3½oz) butter

2 plump pheasants, breasts and leg joints removed

salt and freshly ground black pepper

2 large cooking apples, peeled, cored and thickly sliced

6 shallots, peeled

200ml (7fl oz) Calvados

250ml (8fl oz) crème fraîche

zest and juice of 1 lemon

1 small bunch of tarragon, leaves removed and roughly chopped

Preheat the oven to 180°C/350°F/Gas 4. Heat half the butter in a large heavy-based frying pan. Season the pheasant joints and brown them in the pan until golden on both sides. Remove and set aside.

Heat the remaining butter in the same pan and brown the apple slices until golden. Lay the apple over the base of a shallow, ovenproof casserole dish and arrange the pheasant pieces on top. Deglaze the frying pan with the Calvados, cook it over a high heat until it has reduced by half, then pour the liquid over the pheasant. Cover and cook in the oven for 30 minutes.

Remove from the oven, stir in the crème fraîche, lemon juice and zest, tarragon and seasoning and cook for a further 10 minutes or until the sauce is warmed through.

Orange roulade

This is a colourful, luscious, sticky roulade that has remained popular through the decades. It is best made on the day of serving, but the good news is that it is extremely quick to make.

SERVES 8

4 large eggs, separated

115g (4oz) refined golden caster sugar

zest and juice of 2 large unwaxed oranges

55g (2oz) ground almonds

toasted almond flakes, to decorate

300ml (10fl oz) whipping cream

2 tbsp Grand Marnier or orange liqueur

icing sugar, for dusting

Preheat the oven to 180°C/350°F/Gas 4 and line a roulade tin with greaseproof paper.

In a clean bowl, whisk the egg whites to soft peaks and set aside. In another bowl, whisk the yolks with the sugar until thick and pale. Add the orange zest and juice and whisk in slowly. Carefully fold in the ground almonds and egg whites and pour the mixture into the roulade tin, so it covers the base evenly. Cook for about 20 minutes until golden and firm to the touch.

Remove from the oven and transfer to a wire rack to cool slightly, for about 5 minutes. Set a clean piece of greaseproof paper sprinkled with toasted almond flakes on a flat work surface, then carefully place the roulade upside down onto the paper. Gently pull away the parchment paper, taking care not to take the cooked roulade with it, and carefully roll up the roulade. Chill for 20 minutes.

Whip the cream until thick and fold in the liqueur. Unroll the roulade and spread the cream evenly over the entire roulade. Ideally, select a long, rectangular-shaped plate and place it close to where you are working, then, starting at top end, tightly roll the roulade towards you until it is all rolled up. Carefully transfer it to the plate – it is very soggy and may need to be pushed back into shape. Dust lightly with icing sugar just before serving.

Pecan praline cheesecake

I first made this cheesecake using a friend's recipe in Australia; it is very rich and has been a firm favourite for many years. It is best made a day or two before serving, to allow the flavours to develop. Gingernut biscuits would be a good alternative to digestives, to give the cheesecake a little extra zing.

SERVES 12

Crumb crust

125g (4½oz) digestive biscuits, crushed

60g (2oz) unsalted butter, melted

Filling

750g (1lb 10oz) full-fat cream cheese

2 tsp vanilla extract

150g (5½oz) brown sugar

3 eggs

2 tbsp plain flour

125g (4½oz) finely chopped pecans

Topping

100g (3½oz) soft brown sugar

60g (2oz) butter

300ml (10fl oz) double cream

Pecan praline

100g (3½oz) refined golden caster sugar

2 tbsp water

60g (2oz) pecans

Combine the crushed biscuits and butter in a bowl and mix well. Press over the base of a 23cm (9in) springform pan and chill for 30 minutes.

Preheat the oven to 180°C/350°F/Gas 4. Beat the cream cheese and vanilla until smooth, then add the brown sugar and all the eggs, one at a time. Stir in the flour and pecans and pour the mixture onto the cooled biscuit base. Bake for 45 minutes or until set. Allow to cool, then refrigerate overnight.

For the topping, combine the brown sugar and butter in a pan over a low heat, add the cream and cook, stirring, until smooth and thick. Pour over the set cheesecake filling.

For the praline, stir the sugar and water in a pan over a low heat until the sugar has dissolved. Boil rapidly for about 5 minutes, without stirring, until the mixture turns a light golden brown. Add the pecans and pour the mixture onto a clean, lightly greased baking tray and set aside to cool. Once the praline has set, remove it from the tray and chop it up as finely as you wish, then sprinkle it over the finished cheesecake before serving.

Poached saffron pears

These golden pears are easy to prepare and are delicious served with a warm chocolate sauce or just pure, unadulterated double cream. Choose firm, evenly sized pears for the best texture.

SERVES 8

200g (7oz) refined golden caster sugar

800ml (1¼ pints) water

10 whole cardamom pods, slightly crushed

½ tsp fresh saffron strands

70ml (2½fl oz) freshly squeezed lemon juice

8 firm William or Comice pears, peeled, but stem left on

Put the sugar, water, cardamom pods, saffron and lemon juice into a large, deepish, heavy-based pan, and stand the pears in the syrup. Gently simmer, uncovered, for about an hour, occasionally turning the pears so that the syrup infuses the flesh on all sides and gives them a golden colour. Allow the pears to cool to room temperature in the syrup to enable the colours to intensify.

Remove the pears and set them in a glass dish or individual dishes. Boil the juice to reduce it (if it hasn't already reached a syrupy reduction), then pour it over the pears and leave them to cool. Serve at room temperature.

Apple and blackberry hazelnut crumble

This classic English pudding is perfect when you feel the first chill of autumn in the air, but you can easily substitute seasonal fruits and enjoy this year-round; peaches and apricots in the summer, rhubarb in the spring. If you prefer, replace the hazelnuts with crushed almonds and the blackberries with cranberries for a sharper fix.

SERVES 8

1.3kg (2.8lb) Braeburn apples, peeled, cored, quartered, then sliced again

zest of 1 orange

3 star anise

2 tbsp water

juice of ½ lemon

70g (3oz) light brown unrefined sugar

350g (12oz) blackberries

The crumble

200g (7oz) plain flour

pinch of fine salt

100g (3½oz) unsalted chilled butter, cubed

100g (3½oz) lightly crushed hazelnuts

150g (5½oz) muscovado sugar

pinch of cinnamon

grated nutmeg

Put the apple pieces, orange zest, star anise, water, lemon juice and sugar in a heavy pan over a medium heat and poach the fruit for 5 minutes, tossing the apple pieces occasionally.

Remove the star anise and transfer the fruit to a shallow ovenproof dish, evenly covering its base. Scatter over the blackberries.

Preheat the oven to 190°C/375°F/Gas 5. Put the flour, salt, butter, hazelnuts, 100g (3½oz) of the sugar in a blender and pulse briefly to create a crumble. Scatter this over the fruit and, with the flat of your hand, press it down firmly all over. Sprinkle over the remaining sugar, a little cinnamon and grated nutmeg. Bake in the oven for about 35 minutes until the top is golden brown.

Remove from the oven and allow to rest for 10 minutes before serving with a large dollop of your chosen indulgence!

Decadent Dinners

It's official – eating in is the new going out, and it's easy to serve food as good as you can get in a restaurant if you have a few faithful, foolproof recipes up your sleeve.

A more formal, seated dinner party demands more robust and often more sophisticated food. Three courses and cheese are still the norm, although in these health-conscious times increasingly starters are being replaced with nibbles or appetisers to avoid overindulgence! However you want to entertain, this is your opportunity to really go to town and produce something special. The recipes here can be mixed and matched to suit the mood or time of year, and can be served with a colourful variety of seasonal vegetables.

As with all my recipes, much of the meal can be prepared ahead so you don't spend the whole evening dashing in and out of the kitchen rather than being with your friends.

Duck breasts with honey, ginger and mustard

These are a hit any time of the year and extremely easy to prepare – they just need to be sautéd in the morning and shoved in the oven at the last moment just as your guests are getting hungry. As with all red meat, it is best to leave the duck breasts to rest for a short while before slicing them. These are wonderful served over some steamed bok choy and a good artichoke or garlic and potato purée. As an alternative, cook the duck with a pomegranate molasses mixed with a little runny honey, grain mustard and grated ginger.

SERVES 8

4 spring onions

2 small red chillies

7 very large or 8 medium plump Barbary duck breasts

3 tbsp Dijon mustard

2 tbsp runny honey

5cm (2½in) piece of fresh root ginger, peeled and grated

2 tbsp Fino sherry

8 tbsp orange juice

4 star anise

1 tbsp soy sauce

50g (2oz) chilled butter

salt and freshly ground black pepper

Preheat the oven to 220°C/425°F/Gas 7.

Trim and slice the spring onions lengthways, cut them into thin julienne strips and set them, covered, in a bowl of iced water, where with time they will curl as a perfect topping. Slice the chillies in half lengthways, then remove the seeds and slice very finely. Set aside.

Pat dry the duck breasts, then score the skin diagonally using a sharp knife. Combine the mustard, honey and ginger and pour this over the duck to coat. Set a heavy, ovenproof frying pan over a high heat and sauté the duck, skin-side down, for 3 minutes. Coat the bottom with more of the honey mix, then turn over and cook on the other side for a further 3 minutes. Place the pan in the oven for 10 minutes, then remove and check the duck is pink and cooked – the meat should be springy to the touch. Set the duck breasts aside to rest on a warm plate covered in foil. Drain off any excess fat and stir in the sherry, orange juice, star anise and soy sauce. Boil vigorously to reduce by half. Lower the heat and add the chilled butter, which will give the sauce a shine.

Dry the spring onions on some kitchen paper, carve the duck diagonally and serve with the sauce and spring onion and chilli garnish.

Grilled poussins with orange and Tabasco sauce

This is one of my favourite summer recipes; the flavours are fabulous in the heat and it is so easy to make that I don't need to spend precious summer time in the kitchen. Depending on the size of the poussins, they can be cut in half for each person. I prepare the birds and marinate them overnight, then sauté them in the morning, finishing them off in a hot oven for the last 20 minutes before serving.

Serve these delicious birds over Camargue rice, cooked then fried in a little butter with sliced spring onions and browned pine nuts, topped with a large handful of fresh rocket leaves, or with warm couscous, mixed with roasted tomatoes, mint and chopped flatleaf parsley.

SERVES 6

6 poussins

1 large orange, peeled and roughly chopped

juice of 1 lime

2 tbsp runny honey

1 tbsp Dijon mustard

600ml (1 pint) Greek yoghurt

a splash of Tabasco sauce

2 garlic cloves, roughly chopped

½ small red onion, roughly chopped

1 tbsp toasted cumin seeds

Cut each poussin along its backbone with a sharp heavy knife or kitchen scissors and flatten out the bird with your hand. Place them in an large dish or baking tray.

Place all the remaining ingredients in a liquidizer and blend well for 5 minutes. Pour this marinade over the poussins, making sure the meat is evenly coated, cover the dish and set aside to marinate overnight in the fridge.

When you are ready to cook, preheat the oven to 180°C/350°F/Gas 4 and heat the barbecue or grill. Cook the birds for about 8 minutes on each side, then put them in a clean ovenproof dish with the remaining marinade and place in the oven for a further 20 minutes, basting them occasionally until they are golden on top.

Once cooked, remove the birds from the dish and set aside to rest, covered in foil, for 10 minutes. Pour the sauce from around the chicken into a jug, check the seasoning, and serve warm, spooned over the cooked birds.

Beaujolais chicken

I like to make casseroles a few days in advance, as it allows the meat to become really tender and the flavours to develop, and it also means I can remove any excess fat from the top of the dish before reheating it to make it a slightly healthier meal.

This recipe is my version of a classic coq au vin and is delicious served with mashed potato or any vegetable purée to soak up the rich wine sauce. I like to use chicken thighs; they are dark meat, which has more flavour, and are also inexpensive and a perfect size to serve per person. Another variation is to use 500ml (16fl oz) Riesling with 300ml (10oz) double cream instead of the red wine and brandy.

SERVES 8

24 small shallots, peeled

75g (3oz) butter

175ml (6fl oz) chicken stock

1½ tbsp refined granulated sugar

1 tbsp sunflower oil

250g (9oz) pancetta cubes

salt and freshly ground black pepper

2kg (4½lb) boned chicken thighs

100ml (3½fl oz) brandy

1 x 75cl bottle red Beaujolais or fruity light burgundy

1 bouquet garni (celery, parsley bay leaf and thyme)

1½ tbsp tomato purée

3 garlic cloves, crushed

500g (1lb 2oz) small chestnut mushrooms

1 tbsp plain flour

bunch of flat-leaf parsley, chopped

Place the shallots, butter, stock and sugar in a pan, cover and simmer for about 15 minutes, then uncover and continue to simmer until the liquid has almost evaporated. Coat the shallots well in the caramelised liquid and set aside.

Add the oil to a large pan and fry the pancetta until it is crispy. Set aside. Season the chicken and sauté the pieces, turning them so they are browned on all sides. Set aside, then discard any excess oil. Deglaze the pan with the brandy. Reduce this liquid by half and return the chicken to the pan along with the wine, bouquet garni, tomato purée and garlic. Stir well, cover, and cook over a medium heat for 30 minutes. Add the mushrooms and cook for a further 15 minutes.

Put the flour in a small bowl and add enough of the cooking liquid to blend it to a smooth paste. Add this paste to the chicken mixture and stir well. Remove the bouquet garni and check the seasoning. Set aside to cool, then once completely cool, refrigerate until needed.

Before reheating, preheat the oven to 180°C/350°F/Gas 4 and remove any solid fat from the top using a spoon. Add the shallots and pancetta and place in the oven for 1 hour until heated through and bubbling. Serve with the fresh parsley scattered over.

Lamb korma

The perfect compromise for curry lovers who don't like too much heat. This aromatic, creamy lamb dish is mild but full of flavour and is always extremely popular. Like most casseroles, this is best made 2 days before serving. Serve with a combination of wild and long grain rice, and top with some Caramelised shallot topping (page 154) as an alternative to the flaked almonds, if you prefer.

SERVES 8

2 onions, peeled and roughly chopped

4 garlic cloves

12 whole cardamom pods

50g (2oz) ground almonds

10cm piece of fresh root ginger, peeled and roughly chopped

2½kg (5½lb) good lamb (leg or neck) chopped into 5cm (2in) cubes

200g (7oz) unsalted butter

2 onions, finely sliced

2 cinnamon sticks

4 fresh bay leaves

3 tsp cumin seeds

500ml (16fl oz) natural yoghurt

300ml (10fl oz) double cream

salt and freshly ground black pepper

8 tbsp chopped fresh coriander, to serve

2 tbsp browned flaked almonds, to serve

Place the onions, garlic, cardamom, almonds and ginger in a blender and pulse to form a paste – add a little cold water if needed. Coat the meat well with this mixture and place in the fridge overnight.

The next day, heat the butter in a large pan and brown the sliced onions, then remove and set aside. In the same pan, sauté the meat in batches, without overcrowding, until it is browned on all sides. Return the onion to the pan along with the cinnamon sticks, bay leaves and cumin seeds. Cover with about 200ml (7fl oz) water and simmer for 1 hour, covered.

Mix together the yoghurt, cream and salt and pepper. Stir this into lamb and simmer gently for about another 40 minutes, stirring every 15 minutes, until the lamb is tender. If you have prepared this in advance, reheat by gently simmering for 30 minutes or until it is piping hot.

Check the seasoning – it usually needs a good pinch of salt – and serve with coriander and flaked almonds scattered over.

Lamb tagine

This Middle Eastern-style slow-roasted lamb casserole can be made a few days in advance, and in fact is best prepared this way as the flavour, colour and texture of the dish will benefit enormously. For a truly authentic touch, cook this in a conical tagine dish, but if you don't have one an ordinary casserole dish is perfectly good. Serve with a couscous or rice salad (see Orange and fig couscous, page 115) in large wide bowls topped with a little Salsa verde (page 153).

Heat the oil in a large flameproof casserole dish over a high heat and cook the lamb in batches, without overcrowding, until it is browned all over. Set aside and remove any excess oil from the pan. Lower the heat and cook the onions and garlic until translucent. Return the lamb to the casserole and add the rest of the ingredients, except the coriander and sesame seeds, making sure there is enough liquid to cover the meat. If not, add a little extra water.

Cover the pan and cook on the hob at a steady simmer or in an oven preheated to 160°C/325°F/Gas 3 for 1½ hours or until the lamb is tender. If you have cooked it in advance, reheat, gently simmering it for 30 minutes or until it is piping hot.

Serve with chopped coriander and sesame seeds scattered over or with some salsa verde.

SERVES 8

3 tbsp olive oil

2kg (4½lb) diced leg lamb, seasoned

2 medium onions, diced

4 garlic cloves, crushed

2 tsp ground ginger

2 tbsp fresh chopped tarragon

200ml (7fl oz) water

6 tbsp runny honey

4 tbsp whole blanched almonds

2 tsp harissa paste

4 tsp sea salt

3 tsp cinnamon

125g (4½oz) prunes with stones (they hold their shape better)

2 tbsp chopped coriander, to serve

4 tbsp toasted sesame seeds, to serve

Rich daube of beef

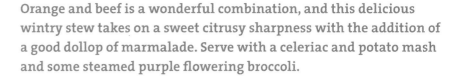

Orange and beef is a wonderful combination, and this delicious wintry stew takes on a sweet citrusy sharpness with the addition of a good dollop of marmalade. Serve with a celeriac and potato mash and some steamed purple flowering broccoli.

SERVES 6

20g (¾oz) dried wild mushrooms (porcini)

4 tbsp olive oil

900g (2lb) piece stewing beef, cut into thick slices, seasoned

225g (8oz) shallots, peeled and skinned

1 tbsp plain flour

3 large garlic cloves, crushed

2.5cm (1in) piece of fresh root ginger, finely grated

125g (4½oz) Roasted cherry plum tomatoes (page 150)

2 tsp mixed dried herbs

300ml (10fl oz) fruity red wine

1 tbsp coarse-cut orange marmalade

Bouquet garni (page 148)

225g (8oz) shiitake mushrooms

small bunch of flatleaf parsley, roughly chopped

Rinse the dried mushrooms under running water, then leave to soak in a bowl filled with 100ml (3½fl oz) cold water for 1 hour.

Heat half the oil in a large flameproof casserole and brown the beef in batches over a fairly high heat. Remove from the pan and set aside. Lower the heat, add a tablespoon of oil and sauté the onions for 10–15 minutes until translucent.

Preheat the oven to 160°C/325°F/Gas 3. Return all the meat to the pan and stir in the flour, garlic, ginger, roasted tomatoes and herbs. Cook, stirring, for 1 minute. Add the wild mushrooms and their soaking liquid, along with the wine and the marmalade. Add the bouquet garni. Cover and bring to the boil, stirring, for 5 minutes. Place in the oven for 2½ hours or until the meat is tender – checking every so often to ensure there is enough liquid, and stir well.

Half an hour before the end of the cooking time, heat the remaining oil in frying pan and cook the shiitake mushrooms over a high heat for 3–4 minutes and add them to the casserole. Taste, and adjust the seasoning if needed, then serve scattered with roughly chopped parsley.

Veal Foyot

This recipe comes from an aunt in Australia who first ate this dish at Restaurant Foyot, in Paris, in 1932. Veal combines well with this delicious crust of Gruyère and breadcrumbs, however, this meat is very lean and so extra care must be taken not to overcook it. This is delicious served hot for dinner or cold for a picnic.

SERVES 10

2 large onions, chopped

30g (1oz) butter

100ml (3½fl oz) dry white wine

100ml (3½fl oz) beef stock

salt and freshly ground black pepper

2kg (4½lb) nut of veal (from the leg), or a rolled loin

200g (7oz) Gruyère cheese, grated

200g (7oz) sourdough breadcrumbs

50g (2oz) butter

1 tin consommé

Gently sauté the onions in the butter in a large pan until translucent. Add the wine and stock with some salt and pepper to taste, then bring to the boil and cook for a few minutes. Remove from the heat.

Preheat the oven to 180°C/350°F/Gas 4. Season the veal with salt and pepper, set it in a large ovenproof dish with plenty of room for basting and surround the meat with the onion mix. Combine the cheese and breadcrumbs with some black pepper and press this mix firmly onto the veal with a heavy knife to form a thick crust – this will prevent the veal drying out. Melt the butter and pour it over the meat, then place the meat in the oven and cook for 2 hours. Baste the meat carefully every 30 minutes, taking care not to disturb the crust. Should the top begin to brown too fast, loosely cover it with some foil. Add the consommé if needed, to stop it drying out. Test the veal with a skewer to see if it is cooked – the juices should run clear.

Set aside to rest for 10 minutes, then carve into thick slices and serve with the sweet braised onion and meat juices.

Lemon-roasted trout with salsa verde

Preparing a whole fish is much easier than most people think. This boning method is simple and should remove any prejudices about eating a fine-boned fish, and the end result makes it well worth the effort. You can buy preserved lemons, such as the Belazu brand, from any good Italian grocer. I like to serve this over some lightly crushed new potatoes or good garlic mash with some fine beans tossed with roasted cherry tomatoes.

SERVES 6

6 whole, medium-sized, fresh trout, scaled, cleaned, gutted and trimmed

small bunch fresh thyme

3 small preserved lemons, quartered

extra virgin olive oil

100ml white wine

Salsa verde, to serve (page 153)

Rinse the fish inside and out and pat dry with kitchen paper. Using a sharp, narrow, filleting knife, cut from the centre of the open belly to the tail. Open out the belly and set the fish, belly down, on a chopping board and firmly press down along the entire spine to release it from the flesh. Turn the fish over, and gently remove the loose spine, taking care to retain the pink flesh. Repeat for all the remaining fish. Cut away the fins using a pair of kitchen scissors and discard.

Preheat the oven to 200°C/400°F/Gas 6. Tuck a whole stalk of thyme and 2 quarters of preserved lemons into each belly cavity. Brush each fish with a little olive oil and season them all over. Set them in a shallow ovenproof dish lined with foil, pour in the wine and bake for 20 minutes, uncovered, basting halfway through cooking.

Serve immediately, topped with a little salsa verde.

Grilled blackened swordfish

I love good meaty fish as it takes stronger flavours so well. In this recipe you can substitute the swordfish for halibut, hake or any meaty fresh fish, if you prefer. This has a bit of a Creole kick, so it is particularly good served with a creamy potato and artichoke mash and a herb leaf salad and lemony vinaigrette, or some sautéed fennel and creamed fresh leaf spinach. It is quick to prepare, and can be made in advance and finished off in a hot oven just before serving.

SERVES 8

2 tsp each of garlic salt, onion powder, cayenne pepper, ground white and black pepper

1 tsp each of dried basil, thyme and sage

100g (3½oz) butter

8 thick swordfish steaks (approximately 175g/6oz each)

2 lemons, quartered, to serve

Preheat the oven to 180°C/350°F/Gas 4.

Mix together the spices and herbs in a large flat bowl. Melt the butter in the microwave or in a pan over a low heat and pour into a shallow bowl. Dip the fish steaks into the butter on both sides, shake off any excess, then lay them onto the herbs mix, coating the fish on both sides.

Set a large frying pan over a high heat and dry sauté the fish on both sides for about 4 minutes until golden. Put the cooked fillets in an ovenproof dish, cover with foil and bake for 12 minutes until just cooked through.

Serve with the lemon quarters to squeeze over.

Celeriac purée

SERVES 8

750g (1lb 10oz) red King Edward or Desiree potatoes, peeled and cubed

1 large celeriac, skin cut off and cut into cubes

1 tsp vinegar

75g (2½oz) butter, plus extra for cooking

3 tbsp crème fraîche

salt, pepper and freshly grated nutmeg

juice of ½ lemon

I adore root vegetables, which is fortunate as they are so in fashion right now, and they are perfect for creating many alternative purées, including leek and potato; swede and carrot; sweet potato with tamari and maple syrup; grilled artichoke hearts and potato; roasted garlic, ground almonds and potato; or cauliflower, garlic and thyme. Root vegetables are perfect served with any meat or fish, and can be prepared in advance then reheated in the microwave or oven. These two purées are among my favourites.

Cook the potatoes in a pan of boiling salted water, drain well and mash roughly. At the same time, cook the celeriac in boiling salted water with the vinegar (to prevent browning) until tender. Drain well and place half the mashed potato and celeriac, the butter, crème fraîche, seasoning, and lemon juice in a blender. Briefly blend, then repeat with the remaining potato and celeriac.

If this is to be reheated in the microwave, make sure it is heated through thoroughly by stirring it every few minutes. Alternatively, reheat it in a moderate oven with a little extra butter added and covered in foil.

Jerusalem artichoke purée

SERVES 8

1.5kg (3lb 3oz) Jerusalem artichokes

4 shallots, peeled and chopped

100g (3½oz) unsalted butter

bunch of fresh thyme, chopped

400ml (14fl oz) white wine

300ml (10fl oz) double cream

salt and freshly ground black pepper

Winter is the season for eating Jerusalem artichokes and good meat casseroles – and the two go beautifully together. This is a creamy, slightly sweet purée which is wonderfully satisfying.

Rinse and scrub clean the artichokes – this is easier than peeling them, which loses too much of the root. Set aside in a bowl of cold water. Gently sweat the shallots in a frying pan in the butter, then add the thyme and white wine and boil until the wine has reduced by half. Slice the artichokes into bite-sized pieces, then add these and the cream to the shallot mix. Cover and simmer gently for 30 minutes until the artichokes are tender.

Blend the mixture in a blender until it is smooth, season to taste and serve.

Savoy cabbage with shallots, lemon and chilli oils

SERVES 6

1 large Savoy cabbage

olive oil and butter, for frying

2 shallots, peeled and finely chopped

1 garlic clove, finely grated

drizzle of chilli oil

zest of 1 lemon

This recipe adds a whole new dimension to cabbage, and will convert even the most staunch haters of this vegetable. This wonderful combination of flavours and colours works perfectly with both meat and fish; the cabbage can be cooked ahead of time then fried with the garlic and flavoured oils just before serving.

Remove and discard any damaged outer leaves from the cabbage, then cut it in half. Cut out the core and finely slice the leaves into ribbons. Bring a large pan of well-salted water to the boil and drop the cabbage into the water. Boil, with the lid on for 2 minutes, then transfer the leaves to a colander and hold under cold running water so that they retain their vibrant colour. Set aside.

Heat a little olive oil and butter in a large frying pan and gently cook the shallots and garlic for about 10 minutes until they are soft. Toss in the cabbage and cook until warmed through, check the seasoning, then serve in a warm dish drizzled with the chilli oil and with lemon zest finely grated over the top.

French peas

SERVES 8

900g (2lb) petit pois

1 tbsp water

1 Little Gem lettuce, sliced

3 shallots, finely sliced

125g (4½oz) butter, plus extra for greasing

2 sprigs of parsley

1 tsp refined sugar

2 sprigs of thyme

salt and freshly ground black pepper

This is the incomparable French method for preparing peas; they are perfect with any dish but especially good with a roast chicken.

In a small pan, cover the peas with the water, lettuce leaves, shallots, butter, parsley, sugar, thyme and salt and pepper. Cover with a buttered piece of greaseproof paper and a lid and cook over a low heat for about 30 minutes or until the liquid is almost totally absorbed.

Fennel and Parmesan gratin

SERVES 8

butter, for greasing

6 large fennel bulbs

450g (1lb) grated Parmesan

sea salt and freshly ground black pepper

a little grated nutmeg

450ml (¾ pint) single cream

I adore fennel – the colour and flavour – and these two fennel dishes are perfect served alongside any fish, chicken or game dish.

Preheat the oven to 180°C/350°F/Gas 4 and grease a shallow ovenproof dish with a little butter.

Remove any old leaves from the fennel and trim both ends of the bulbs. Slice the bulbs vertically into 2.5cm (1in) pieces, cutting out the hard base. Place the fennel chunks in a pan of boiling salted water and cook for 2 minutes. Drain, then run under cold water for a minute or two, to preserve their colour, then leave to drain very well before transferring them to a piece of kitchen paper.

Put the fennel in the greased dish and sprinkle with half the Parmesan, salt and pepper and nutmeg and pour over the cream. Sprinkle over the remaining Parmesan. Bake in the centre of the oven for 30–40 minutes or until the top is golden.

Baked fennel and red onions with garlic butter and vermouth

SERVES 8

4 large fennel bulbs

3 large red onions

50g (2oz) butter

1 garlic clove, finely sliced

1 glass of vermouth

1 tbsp red wine vinegar

1 tbsp brown sugar

1 tbsp olive oil

salt and freshly ground black pepper

Preheat the oven to 200°C/400°F/Gas 6. Remove any bruised outer leaves from the fennel and cut the bulb lengthways into six slices, removing the bottom and tops as well as the core in centre.

Peel the onions and cut into six slices, the same size as fennel. Put all the ingredients into a shallow baking dish, cover with foil and bake for 30 minutes (to both bake and steam the vegetables at the same time).

Raise the oven temperature to 220°C/425°F/Gas 7, remove the foil and cook for a further 30 minutes or until the vegetables have absorbed the liquid and begun to caramelise.

Gratin dauphinois

This is a trusted old recipe that never fails to please, but I have adapted it by adding a hint of cinnamon and some gooey Gruyère. The trick to getting the perfect texture is to use firm waxy potatoes and to cook them just long enough that they brown but don't dry out. Sweet potatoes make a good alternative to regular potatoes in this classic dish, but omit the cinnamon or nutmeg.

SERVES 10

1.4kg (3lb) Desiree or King Edward potatoes

1 sprig of rosemary, leaves stripped and roughly chopped

150g (5½oz) Gruyère, grated

a little grated nutmeg

salt and freshly ground black pepper

pinch of cinnamon

200ml (7fl oz) double cream

300ml (10fl oz) milk

3 garlic cloves, finely grated

150g (5½oz) grated Parmesan

Preheat the oven to 150°C/300°F/Gas 2. Peel and finely slice the potatoes, then rinse them under cold water in a colander. Leave to drain, then transfer to kitchen paper.

Discard the knobbly ends of the sliced potatoes and make one layer of potato slices in the baking dish. Sprinkle over some of the rosemary with some of the Gruyère, grated nutmeg, salt and pepper. Continue the layers in the same fashion, sprinkling some cinnamon on the last layer.

Heat the cream, milk and garlic gently over a low heat, then pour this mix over the layers to just below the top of the potatoes. Cover with foil and bake for 1½ hours. After this time, remove the foil and sprinkle over the Parmesan. Increase the heat to 190°C/375°F/Gas 5, return to the oven and bake for a further 30 minutes until the gratin is delicately browned.

Either serve entire in its dish or, using a large round pastry cutter and palette knife, carefully cut out rounds to serve alongside meat or fish.

Orange and fig couscous

This healthy, colourful salad is particularly good with grilled lamb on a warm summer's day, but will also brighten up a dreary day at any other time of year. Make it ahead or make extra, as it will keep for several days in a sealed container in the fridge.

SERVES 8

good pinch of saffron strands

250g (9oz) couscous

25g (1oz) melted butter

600ml (1 pint) hot vegetable stock

2 large oranges

100g (3½oz) raisins

1 tbsp extra virgin olive oil

salt and freshly ground black pepper

1 pomegranate

4 fresh figs

1 tbsp soft brown sugar

50g (2oz) toasted pine nuts

small bunch flatleaf parsley, roughly chopped

Gently rub the saffron strands between your fingers into a small ramekin and cover with a tablespoon of hot water to release the colour and flavour.

Place the couscous, saffron and water along with the melted butter in a large bowl and pour over enough of the hot stock to barely cover the couscous. Set aside to absorb the liquid and expand. After about 12 minutes, fork through the mixture to break up any lumps and add the finely grated zest from 1 of the oranges, along with the raisins and olive oil and seasoning.

Roll the pomegranate to loosen the seeds, cut it in half horizontally and scoop out the seeds into the couscous. Next, with a very sharp small knife, skin the remaining orange along with the pith and membrane. Slice each segment from the orange and toss them into the couscous.

Preheat the grill to Medium. Quarter the figs then set them on a baking tray, sprinkle them with brown sugar and lightly caramelise them under the grill. Set aside to cool.

Spoon out the couscous into an attractive dish and top with the figs, pine nuts and parsley.

Caramelised chicory with orange, breadcrumbs and roasted prosciutto

I love to create beautiful and appealing vegetables with a rustic feel that will go well with any fish or meat dishes. This is one such idea; it is full of interesting flavours and has a sweet but bitter taste. This is perfect for a light lunch when served at room temperature with a little crunchy leaf salad on the side. Any cured ham – Parma, Serrano or Bayonne – can be used.

A delicious variation is to bake the chicory with a few rinsed capers and some chopped red chillies, drizzled with olive oil. Cook for 30 minutes at 180°C/350°F/Gas 4.

SERVES 8

4 large, very fresh chicory heads

75g (2½oz) butter

75g (2½oz) soft, dark brown refined sugar

200g (7oz) sourdough coarse breadcrumbs

zest and juice of 1 small orange

200g (7oz) grated Gran Padano cheese

6 sprigs of fresh thyme, leaves shredded from the stalks

salt and freshly ground black pepper

8 large slices of good prosciutto

Preheat the oven to 200°C/400°F/Gas 6.

Cut the chicory heads horizontally down the middle and remove any bruised outer leaves. Gently heat the butter in a large frying pan and add the sugar. Raise the heat until the butter and sugar are mixed together and press the chicory firmly into the pan, cut-side down. Lower the heat a little and leave for about 6 minutes to caramelise. Turn the chicory pieces very carefully and sauté them on the opposite side.

Line an ovenproof dish with foil and set the sautéed chicory cut-side up in it.

Mix the breadcrumbs in a bowl with the orange juice and zest, cheese, thyme leaves, salt and pepper. Mix well using your hands and carefully stuff this mixture between the leaves and the top of the chicory. Lay a slice of prosciutto over each piece and bake in the oven for 20 minutes until it is crispy.

Crème brulée with blackberries

Crème brulée is such a classic, and this recipe is so easy to make. If you have a blender, it's even easier and, as I've discovered from experience, making it this way means it has little chance of curdling. The pudding can be set in individual ramekins or in a large soufflé dish up to a day in advance, then bruléed before serving.

SERVES 8

600ml (1 pint) double cream

1 vanilla pod

4 egg yolks

100g (3½oz) refined caster sugar

11g sachet gelatine

250g (9oz) fresh blackberries

Gently heat the cream in a pan until it is boiling and remove from the heat. Slice the vanilla pod lengthways and scoop out the seeds, using the tip of a knife, into the warm cream.

Beat the egg yolks and half the sugar together in a blender until pale and creamy. With the motor running, gradually pour in the hot cream. Dissolve the gelatine following the instructions on the packet, stirring until it is totally dissolved and clear, then set aside to cool. Transfer the cream from the blender back into the pan and cook, stirring constantly, over a very low heat until the custard begins to thicken – this may take 10–15 minutes – but do not let it boil. Remove from the heat and continue to stir for a further 5 minutes, then stir in the gelatine. Leave to cool, stirring every few minutes.

Place a few blackberries in the bottom of each ramekin or over the base of a large soufflé dish and pour the custard over. Cover with cling film and chill for a minimum of 2 hours until set.

Sprinkle the remaining sugar over the top of the chilled creams and caramelise under a preheated hot grill for a couple of seconds or using a blow torch. Chill before serving.

Lemon tart

Slightly sharp-tasting, this creamy tart is wonderfully refreshing and is perfect to follow a rich meat casserole. It looks wonderful served with fresh mixed berries and accompanied by a dollop of very good crème fraîche. This recipe can also be adapted to make canapé-sized tarts – this quantity of ingredients would make about 50 small tarts.

SERVES 8

300g (10oz) plain flour, plus extra for dusting

fine salt

250g (9oz) refined golden caster sugar

250g (9oz) softened unsalted butter

4 eggs

2 tbsp lemon marmalade

3 tbsp crème fraîche

zest of 1 orange

zest and juice of 2 lemons

icing sugar, for dusting

Line a 28cm (11in) loose-bottomed tart tin with greaseproof paper and preheat the oven to 180°C/350°F/Gas 4.

Whisk together the flour, a pinch of salt, 50g (2oz) of the sugar and 150g (5½oz) of the butter in a blender until it resembles breadcrumbs. Carefully add a little iced water a spoonful at a time until the pastry forms one large ball of dough. On a well-floured surface, knead and roll out the pastry to fit the tin. Transfer to the tin and mould it into the sides, leaving a little pastry hanging over the sides (you can trim this off later). Prick the base of the pastry and set it aside in the fridge for 20 minutes to allow it to shrink. Transfer the tin to the oven and bake blind for 15 minutes. Set aside to cool.

Using the blender, cream together the remaining butter and sugar. Beat the eggs and add them to the cream mix along with the marmalade, crème fraîche and citrus zests. Add the lemon juice – do not be alarmed if the mixture looks curdled at this point, this is quite normal. Set the pastry case onto a baking tray and ladle in the lemon cream carefully. Bake in the oven for 45–50 minutes or until set. Cool, then dust with sieved icing sugar and caramelise briefly under a hot grill.

Praline and
white chocolate ice cream

This ice cream is delicious served with some slightly tart stewed plums or apricots. It is a little more time consuming to make than my other desserts, but it can be made well in advance and kept in the freezer for up to a month. Take care when making the praline that it does not over caramelise, and do not stir it or it will crystallise. Serve in large, pretty, coloured glasses.

SERVES 10

For the praline

225g (8oz) blanched whole almonds

125g (4½oz) refined golden caster sugar

sunflower oil, for greasing

For the ice cream

300g (10oz) white chocolate, broken into pieces

800ml (1¼ pints) double cream, lightly whipped

8 egg yolks

200g (7oz) refined golden caster sugar

120ml (4fl oz) water

(this recipe includes raw egg, so do not serve it to vulnerable groups, such as pregnant women and old people)

First make the praline. Toast the almonds in a large dry frying pan set over a gentle heat for 4–5 minutes until golden. Set aside. Place the sugar and 4 tablespoons of water in the frying pan and, over a gentle heat, let the sugar dissolve. Turn up the heat, add the almonds and, without stirring, cook the mixture to a caramel colour. Pour onto an oiled flat pan and leave to cool and harden.

Roughly break the hardened praline into pieces, setting aside 10 small pieces for decoration. Place the remaining praline in a blender and pulse a few times until it resembles coarse breadcrumbs.

Break the chocolate into a microwaveable bowl and cook on Medium for 4 minutes, or put in a heatproof bowl set over a pan of simmering water, stirring until melted. Set aside to cool completely.

In a clean bowl, whisk the cream to soft peaks and set aside. In a separate bowl, whisk the egg yolks until pale and fluffy. Meanwhile, place the sugar and water in a saucepan over a low heat to dissolve the sugar, increase the heat and boil it until it becomes a sticky syrup. Pour the warmed syrup into the egg mixture in a steady stream with the whisk beating, and continue to beat for 5 minutes so the mixture becomes a pale custard colour. Stir in the melted chocolate and the praline crumbs. Leave to cool completely, then fold in the whisked cream.

Pour into a freezerproof container with a lid and freeze for 5 or 6 hours or until set.

White chocolate and ginger mousse with blueberries

This is another popular and dead-easy pudding. The fresh root ginger takes away some of the sweetness of the white chocolate, giving it a slightly peppery kick, and the blueberries provide a good colour contrast – but you can use any berry that you wish or is in season. The longer the mousse is left in the fridge, the harder it will set, so ideally eat within 4 hours of making.

SERVES 8

200g (7oz) good-quality white chocolate, broken into small pieces

½ x 12 gelatine sachet

300ml (10fl oz) whipping cream

2 large egg yolks

100g (3½oz) icing sugar

6cm piece of fresh root ginger

1 punnet of blueberries

4 stem ginger biscuits, to serve

(this recipe includes raw egg, so do not serve it to vulnerable groups, such as pregnant women and old people)

Break the chocolate into a microwaveable bowl and cook on Medium for 4 minutes or until melted, or put it in a heatproof bowl set over a pan of simmering water – pay particular attention to white chocolate as it overheats much quicker than other chocolates and can become spoiled. Set aside to cool.

Dissolve the gelatine and about 3 tablespoons of the cream in a pan set over a low heat, stirring well until it is totally dissolved – but do not let it boil. Set aside to cool slightly.

In a large bowl, whisk the remaining cream until it is thick, then set aside. Whisk the egg yolks and icing sugar together until thick and pale and add the cooled melted chocolate and dissolved gelatine. Grate the root ginger into the mixture – only add enough to taste, you may not need it all. Fold the whipped cream into the cooled chocolate mix.

Put a handful of blueberries into some individual glass dishes and spoon the chocolate mousse over the top. Place in the fridge for at least 2 hours until chilled and set.

To serve, crush the ginger biscuits roughly in a plastic bag and sprinkle the crumbs over each mousse.

Chocolate fix

No matter how delicious or satisfying a supper, we all have the need for a chocolate fix at the end of an evening. Here are four different chocolate puddings that will satisfy any chocoholic. The first and simplest is one that my mother served for dinner parties in the 1960s, in miniature antique coffee cups, while the last two are the more modern alternatives to ice cream – the semifreddo. All are extremely popular and have been collected and served throughout my travels.

Serving decadent chocolate puddings with fresh mixed berries, red berry compote or a good crème fraîche will help to cut the richness of these desserts – and ease the calorific guilt!

Rich dark chocolate mousse

Break the chocolate into a microwaveable bowl with the butter and cook on High for 4 minutes, or put in a heatproof bowl set over a pan of simmering water. Set aside to cool completely.

Once the chocolate is cool, add the beaten egg yolks, a few drops of vanilla essence, the Grand Marnier and finally the whipped cream. Gently fold in to evenly combine. Pour or spoon the mixture into individual serving pots and set aside in the fridge to set for at least 2 hours.

Remove from the fridge 1 hour before serving to bring up to room temperature and serve with fresh raspberries.

SERVES 8

250g (9oz) good-quality dark chocolate (ideally 70% cocoa solids)

25g (1oz) unsalted butter

2 egg yolks, at room temperature, beaten

vanilla essence

1 tbsp Grand Marnier

300ml (½ pint) whipping cream, whipped

raspberries, to serve

(this recipe includes raw egg, so do not serve it to vulnerable groups, such as pregnant women and old people) safflower or sunflower oil, for greasing

140g pot liquid glucose

250g (9oz) dark chocolate, broken into pieces

2 tbsp Cointreau or Grand Marnier

300ml (10fl oz) whipping cream

150g (5½oz) Amaretti biscuits, or 3 Crunchie bars, crushed

white chocolate, to serve

mixed fresh berries, to serve

SERVES 6

75g (3oz) blanched almonds, chopped

400g (14oz) dark chocolate, chopped

400g (14oz) milk chocolate, chopped

4 eggs

100g (4oz) refined granulated sugar

600ml (1 pint) whipping cream

2 tbsp Grand Marnier

(this recipe includes raw egg, so do not serve it to vulnerable groups, such as pregnant women and old people)

Rich dark chocolate torte

Lightly oil a 20cm (8in) round, loose-bottomed cake tin. Put the glucose and chocolate into a microwaveable bowl and cook on High for 4 minutes, or put in a heatproof bowl set over a pan of simmering water. Stir in the Cointreau and set aside to cool completely.

In a clean bowl, whip the cream and gently fold into the cooled chocolate. Using a rubber spatula, transfer the mixture into the tin, cover with the crushed biscuits, pressing the crumbs firmly into the chocolate. Place in the freezer for 3 hours or until needed.

Remove the torte from the tin using a palette knife, turning the tin upside down over a plate and pushing the loose bottom through the tin carefully. Place the torte in the fridge so that it softens a little before serving.

To serve, coarsely grate some white chocolate over the top and scatter some mixed berries around the side.

Double chocolate and almond ice cream

Line the base of a 23cm (9in) springform pan with foil, so that it is 2.5cm (1in) or so up the sides. Toast the almonds in a dry frying pan until they are golden, then set aside to cool.

Melt the dark chocolate and the milk chocolate in two separate heatproof bowls set over a pan of simmering water. Cool, but do not allow to set.

Beat the eggs and sugar in a bowl until thick, pale and creamy. In a separate bowl, beat the cream until firm peaks form, then fold in the Grand Marnier and almonds and the egg mixture. Divide the mixture between two mixing bowls. Stir the dark chocolate into one and the milk chocolate into the other. Pour the milk chocolate mixture into the tin and place in the freezer for 1 hour or until almost set. Remove from the freezer, top with the dark chocolate mixture, then freeze overnight.

300g (10oz) dark chocolate biscuits

50g (2z) unsalted butter, melted

75ml (2½fl oz) liquid glucose

60ml (2fl oz) water

75g (2½oz) caster sugar

250g (9oz) dark chocolate,
plus extra for grating over

250g (9oz) white chocolate

450ml (15fl oz) whipping cream

1 egg white

(this recipe includes raw egg, so do
not serve it to vulnerable groups, such
as pregnant women and old people)

Rich white and dark chocolate semifreddo

Preheat the oven to 180°C/350°F/Gas 4 and line the bottom of a
25cm (10in) springform tin with greaseproof paper.

Whizz the biscuits in a blender to fine breadcrumbs. Combine with the
butter and press this mixture firmly around the bottom of the cake tin,
then bake for about 15 minutes. Remove from the oven and set aside to
cool completely.

Gently heat the glucose, water and caster sugar in a pan over a low heat,
then bring to the boil. Melt the dark chocolate and the white chocolate
in two separate heatproof bowls set over pans of simmering water – pay
particular attention to the white chocolate as it overheats quicker than
the dark and can burn. Remove from the heat, divide the glucose mixture
evenly between the two bowls, then set aside and leave to cool completely.

In a separate bowl, whip the cream until thick. Beat the egg white until soft
peaks form. Divide the the cream and egg white evenly between the two
chocolate mixtures and fold in.

Pour half the dark chocolate over the biscuit base and freeze for
20 minutes. Then pour half the white chocolate over the dark chocolate
and freeze again for 20 minutes. Repeat this process again, finishing with
a layer of white chocolate.

When ready to serve, use a palette knife to remove the semifreddo from
the tin and serve with a little dark chocolate grated over.

Moveable Feasts

Is there anything more quintessentially English than a picnic?
Eating outdoors adds a whole new dimension to food and is a lovely
way to while away an afternoon or a warm summer evening.

However, not all food travels well, so you need to be a little more
discerning in your choices if you want to avoid a mushy mess as you
open your basket. Having lived in the UK and picnicked in glorious
English countryside, and spent hot days on Australian beaches and
balmy evenings along the coastline of Martha's Vineyard, I have
accumulated quite a collection of recipes that work well in any
outdoor dining situation.

Here I've included my favourite recipes for moveable feasts; food
that can be easily packed up and eaten simply with a fork or just
fingers. It is a varied list of recipes that should satisfy any taste.
Include as many as you like or simply pack up one or two dishes
in a large basket with a variety of hard and soft cheeses, unusual
crackers, spiced crisp pittas, dried apricots and perhaps a pot of
spicy, fruit chutney-style jam from a good deli. And don't forget
the corkscrew!

Coriander and garlic chicken paillade

I created this recipe many years ago but it is still a favourite. A paillade is quite simply meat, usually pork, chicken, turkey, veal or beef, that has been pounded thin and cooked over a grill. This technique tenderises the meat and means it cooks faster – which is perfect for a barbecue.

On a rainy day at home, try wrapping these fillets around a stuffing. Perhaps mozzarella, pesto, goat's cheese, oven-roasted tomatoes or caramelised red onions (the list is endless) in the middle of the escalope, then fold over the sides to create a parcel. Sear these in a hot frying pan to seal the meat, then bake them in the oven at 180°C/350°F/Gas 4 for 15 minutes with a little wine to stop the meat drying out. The cooked paillades can be kept in the fridge for up to four days.

Lay the chicken fillets on a large chopping board and carefully slice through the thickest part horizontally to open out the fillet. Gently pound the chicken, starting at this thickest point and working towards the edges, until you have a fillet of even thickness all over. Peel and crush the garlic into a large dish, and add the lemon and lime zests and juices. Roughly chop the coriander, including the stalks, then add the olive oil, Tabasco and some salt to taste.

In a non-metallic bowl, coat the chicken on both sides with the marinade and leave to marinate, covered, overnight in the fridge.

Cook the meat with its marinade on a barbecue or in a griddle pan for 4 minutes on each side. Serve immediately or leave to cool before packaging up for a picnic.

SERVES 8

8 medium chicken fillets, skinned

3 garlic cloves

zest and juice of 3 lemons

zest and juice of 2 limes

large bunch of coriander, washed and drained

2 tbsp extra virgin olive oil

splash of Tabasco

salt

Coronation chicken

Everyone has their own version of this cold chicken classic – this is mine. I adapted this from the old-fashioned method of making it with a red wine and onion sauce. This sauce can then be frozen just before you add the mayonnaise and yoghurt, although is much better when freshly made. Serve with a good rice salad, such as the Curried wild rice and cashew salad on page 133, or a radicchio and endive salad.

SERVES 6

1 large corn fed organic chicken

Bouquet garni (page 148)

5cm (2in) piece of ginger, peeled and sliced, plus another 2cm (¾in) piece, peeled and finely grated

½ lemon, sliced

1 leek, sliced

1 onion, sliced

3 garlic cloves, peeled, plus 2 finely chopped

10 peppercorns

1 star anise

1 small onion, chopped

1 tbsp olive oil

1 tbsp curry powder

3 tbsp red wine

bay leaf

juice of ½ lemon

1 tbsp tomato purée

salt and freshly ground pepper

125g (4½oz) good-quality mayonnaise (bought, such as Hellmann's, is fine)

2 tbsp good-quality mango chutney, puréed until smooth

3 celery sticks, chopped

100g (3½oz) Greek yoghurt

125g (4½oz) toasted almonds

Cut the chicken in half completely down its breastbone (this will help it to poach faster). Put the chicken halves in a large pan with enough water to completely cover it, then add the bouquet garni, 5cm (2in) piece of ginger, lemon, leek, whole garlic cloves, peppercorns and star anise. Cover and poach over a medium to low heat for 45 minutes. Leave to cool completely in the pan with the lid on.

In a frying pan, gently fry the onion, chopped garlic and grated ginger in the oil until soft. Stir in the curry powder and cook for 1–2 minutes, then add the wine and bay leaf. Bring to the boil. Stir in the lemon juice, tomato purée and seasoning. Simmer for 10 minutes, then remove from the heat and pass through a fine sieve into large mixing bowl. Set aside and leave to cool completely.

Remove the skin and all the fat from the chicken and tear the best meat into large chunks. Stir the mayonnaise, mango chutney, celery and yoghurt into the wine sauce and pour over the chicken. Chill completely, then serve with toasted almonds sprinkled over the top.

Parmesan and chorizo loaf

SERVES 8

1 Vienna loaf or use a stoneground sourdough

185g (6oz) unsalted butter, at room temperature

125g (4½oz) good-quality chorizo, finely chopped

100g (3½oz) grated Parmesan

3 tbsp chopped basil

This is ideal for keeping in the freezer on standby for picnics and barbeques during the busy summer months. Wrap the uncooked loaf in foil and freeze for up to 3 months. If you're taking this on a picnic, heat it first, then wrap it in foil and an extra layer of newspaper to keep it warm.

For a variation, spread the loaf with any of the herb butters listed on page 154.

Preheat the oven to to 180°C/350°F/Gas 4.

Slice the bread crossways at 1cm (½in) intervals, cutting nearly all the way through to the board. Mix the butter well with the chorizo, Parmesan and basil and liberally spread the mixture between each slice. Wrap in foil and bake in the oven for 20–30 minutes.

Open the foil, completely slice the loaf and serve, or re-wrap for a picnic.

Salmon en croute with asparagus and basil cream

This was a lunch I made many times for Estée Lauder® long-service lunches (catering for about 80 people). It looked beautiful when sliced thickly and showing all its wonderful colours, was easy to eat with a fork standing up and has never dated. It is a simple recipe that is best made in the morning or even the day before serving. As an alternative to basil and asparagus, you could fill it with spinach and a cream cheese, such as Boursin. This is perfect for a picnic – day or night.

SERVES 6

250g (9oz) asparagus spears, trimmed

1kg (2¼lb) salmon or trout fillet, skinned

500g (1lb 2oz) puff pastry

flour, for dusting

large handful of basil

100ml (3½fl oz) extra-thick double cream

sea salt and freshly ground black pepper

sunflower oil, for greasing

1 egg, beaten, for glazing

sprigs of watercress, to garnish

Cook the asparagus in a pan of boiling salted water for 2 minutes until just tender. Tip into a colander and rinse under cold running water to preserve the colour, then leave to drain and cool.

Remove any fine bones from the fish fillet, then cut it in half so that you are left with two even lengths. Roll out the pastry on a floured surface; it should be a large, rectangular shape, slightly wider than and twice the length of the fish fillets.

Place the asparagus, basil, cream and salt and pepper in a blender and pulse briefly to roughly chop the mix. Preheat the oven to 200°C/400°F/Gas 6.

Lightly oil a large baking tray and set half the pastry onto it. Lay one piece of fish along one side of the piece of pastry (leaving enough to the other side to fold over and make a parcel), then spoon the asparagus mix into the centre of the fish and cover with the second fish fillet. Season the top salmon fillet lightly with salt and pepper. Fold the remaining pastry over the top of the fish. Trim any excess pastry, leaving just enough to roll inwards to seal the edges and make a parcel.

Using a little beaten egg, brush between the two edges to seal. Brush the top with the remaining egg and cut two air vents in the top of the pastry. Cook in the oven for 30 minutes until the pastry is golden brown.

Remove and cool for 1 hour before slicing into thick 7.5cm (3in) slices – you can cut these in half if you wish. Serve garnished with sprigs of watercress.

Curried wild rice and cashew salad

This is a good, easy, colourful rice salad to serve for large numbers. It is at its best made the day before eating, with the dressing tossed in just before serving.

SERVES 8

400g (14oz) mixed wild and brown long grain rice

2 tbsp olive oil

1 medium onion, finely chopped

2 garlic cloves, finely chopped

2 tsp curry powder

2 tsp black mustard seeds

85g (3oz) sultanas

85g (3oz) dried cranberries

135g (5oz) unsalted roasted cashews, chopped

2 medium carrots, grated

1 small red pepper, chopped and deseeded

1 large apple, peeled and grated

3 spring onions, finely chopped

20g (¾oz) chopped fresh parsley

Dressing

1 egg yolk

2 tbsp cider vinegar

250ml (8fl oz) olive oil

3 tsp curry powder

(this recipe includes raw egg, so do not serve it to vulnerable groups, such as pregnant women and old people)

Cook the rice in a pan of boiling water for about 25 minutes until just tender. Drain well and leave to cool.

Heat the oil in a frying pan and cook the onion, garlic, curry powder and mustard seeds until the onion is soft. Set aside to cool.

In a large jar, combine the dressing ingredients and shake well.

Combine the rice with all the other ingredients. Pour over the dressing and toss well just before serving.

Barbecued Romano peppers with courgette and goat's cheese

Romano peppers are long bell peppers; I have found them in most countries and they are a wonderful accompaniment to any meat or fish in the summer months. This dish can be prepared a day ahead and eaten at room temperature, or if you're eating these at home you can reheat them briefly in the microwave for 2–3 minutes.

SERVES 4

4 medium Romano peppers
(red, orange and yellow)

olive oil, for frying

2 large courgettes, finely sliced

2 garlic cloves, peeled and crushed

125g (4½oz) buffalo mozzarella,
torn into pieces

100g (3½oz) goat's cheese,
roughly chopped

2 tbsp fresh mint leaves

2 spring onions, finely sliced

zest and juice of 1 lemon

2 tbsp pitted black olives, chopped

2 tbsp flatleaf parsley, chopped

Preheat the oven to 180°C/350°F/Gas 4. Place the peppers on a baking tray and roast in the oven for 5 minutes to soften. Remove from the oven and leave to cool. Cut a 5cm (2in) slit down one side of each, open out the peppers and gently scoop out the seeds, taking care not to damage the shape of the peppers.

Heat a tablespoon of olive oil in a frying pan and cook the courgettes over a medium heat for 10 minutes until soft. Add the garlic and cook for 5 more minutes until they begin to brown slightly.

Remove the pan from the heat and mix in the mozzarella, goat's cheese, mint, spring onions, lemon zest and juice. Fill each pepper with the stuffing and secure each one with two cocktail sticks. Char-grill or barbecue the peppers for 5 minutes on each side.

Carefully take the peppers off the heat and leave to cool slightly before removing the cocktail sticks. Serve at room temperature with the chopped olives and parsley.

Pan bagna

If there is one single food that reminds me of my childhood summers it would be this hearty salade niçoise sandwich. We were packed off to the beach by our mother with this as our sustenance for the entire day. Ideally the bread should be a hearty country loaf that is relatively flat and has a crispy crust and plenty of flavour – you can use a plain or olive ciabatta if you wish. The flavours of this sandwich are better if this is made the night before eating (up to about 12 hours in advance).

SERVES 1 HUNGRY PERSON

1 small/medium good-quality loaf

1 garlic clove, cut in half

1 tbsp red wine vinegar

5 tbsp olive oil

1 tbsp Dijon mustard

100g (3½oz) anchovy fillets, coarsely chopped

salt and freshly ground black pepper

4 ripe plum tomatoes

1 small bunch of basil

1 tsp refined sugar

2 hard-boiled eggs, shelled and quartered

1 tbsp sliced fresh olives

125g (4½oz) tin of tuna, drained

1 red pepper, chargrilled, skinned, deseeded and sliced

1 red onion, sliced

1 Little Gem lettuce, sliced

Cut the loaf in half horizontally. Pull out enough of the soft bread to make a large cavity on both sides to hold the filling. Rub the inside surfaces of the loaf with the cut sides of the garlic cloves. Whisk together the vinegar, oil, mustard, anchovies and seasoning, mashing the anchovies into the mix. Drizzle a little of this on both cut sides of the bread.

Skin the tomatoes by first plunging them into a bowl of boiling water and making a cross on top, then cut them into thick slices. Set these on the bread and scatter over the basil and sugar. Load on all the other ingredients, drizzle with any remaining vinaigrette, season to taste with salt and pepper and top with the other piece of the loaf. Press down firmly and secure the sandwich with a rubber band. Wrap in foil and place in the fridge with some weighted object on top to compact the filling.

Trofie with crisp Parma ham, broad beans, ricotta and mint

This is a quick, light and fresh lunch to prepare, and one that is easy to transport and eat on any beach. I discovered something similar whilst staying in Portofino; and this recipe echoes all the warmth and vibrant colours of this special town on the Ligurian coast. If you can't get trofie pasta, use fresh shell or fusilli pasta shapes instead.

SERVES 6

325g (11oz) baby broad beans

3 tbsp minted oil (page 149)

500g (1lb 2oz) trofie pasta

450g (1lb) Parma ham

olive oil

salt and freshly ground black pepper

300g (10oz) fresh ricotta

zest of 1 lemon and juice of ½

80g (2½oz) Parmesan, grated

small handful mint leaves, roughly torn

Place a saucepan of salted water on to boil, and once boiling steadily add the broad beans. Cook for 30 seconds, drain, and refresh under cold water. Drain well and peel off the greyish skins. Cover with 1 tablespoon minted oil and set aside.

Preheat the oven to 190°C/375°F/Gas 5. Cook the pasta in plenty of boiling salted water until al dente. Lay the Parma ham on a baking tray and drizzle with a little oil, then place in the oven for 10 minutes or until crisp.

Mix the ricotta with lemon zest and juice, Parmesan, 1 teaspoon minted oil and salt and pepper to taste. Drain the pasta well and toss with the minted beans, crisp Parma ham torn into pieces and the ricotta. Drizzle with extra minted oil and an extra squeeze of lemon and scatter over the mint leaves.

Cuban corn

SERVES 8

8 corn on cobs (in their husks, for extra freshness)

mayonnaise (Hellmann's is good)

225g (8oz) grated Parmesan cheese

4 limes

Tabasco sauce

This is not so much a recipe as a delicious and easy combination. We lived above a popular Cuban restaurant in New York and this is my adaptation of what we saw being served. The corns can be prepared ahead and wrapped in foil individually to keep warm and be eaten anywhere with the lime and Tabasco at the last minute.

Peel the corns and cook them in a pan of boiling salted water for 2 minutes. Drain, then grill over a barbecue or a hot griddle pan for a few minutes on all sides. Scatter the Parmesan over a plate, then spread the warm corns thickly with mayonnaise and roll them in the Parmesan.

Microwave each lime for 6 seconds, or roll it firmly under your palm on a work surface to loosen the flesh. Cut the limes in half and squeeze over the corns, then splash with a little Tabasco to taste.

Minted pea salad

SERVES 8

500g (1lb 2oz) frozen petit pois

1 tbsp grated fresh root ginger

5 spring onions, sliced

1 garlic clove, crushed

2 tbsp sliced black olives

1 red pepper, deseeded and finely cubed

125g (4½oz) mixed peel

1 tbsp olive oil

10 drops of Tabasco

3 tbsp roughly chopped mint leaves

This recipe is adapted from a very old friend's recipe and is truly a favourite of my husband, Charlie. It's a brilliant all-rounder and works well with any cold or barbecued meat, poultry or fish.

Add all the ingredients except the mint to a large saucepan and cook over a medium heat, covered, for about 10 minutes, stirring occasionally until the red pepper and onions are just soft.

Once cooked, transfer the peas mix to a suitable dish which will show off the colours to their best advantage, then gently stir in the chopped mint and allow everything to cool completely before serving.

Spiced potato salad with coriander and lime

A perfect summer accompaniment for any meat or fish dish. The colours and Eastern flavours of my recipe give a nice twist to the popular, yet perhaps slightly blander, classic potato salad.

SERVES 8

1kg (2¼lb) small new potatoes (Jersey Royals, Anya or Pink Fir Apple are my favourites)

2 garlic cloves, roughly chopped

½ green chilli, chopped (more if you prefer more heat)

2.5cm (1in) piece of fresh ginger, peeled and roughly chopped

½ tsp turmeric

4 tbsp sunflower oil

3 tsp cumin seeds

salt and freshly ground black pepper

100ml (3½fl oz) yoghurt

large bunch of coriander, roughly chopped

zest and juice of 2 limes

Cook the potatoes, whole, in boiling salted water until soft, then drain well. Once cool enough to handle, cut them in half.

Combine the garlic, chilli, ginger and turmeric in a blender with 3 or 4 tablespoons of water to form a paste.

Heat the oil in a wok or large frying pan, add the cumin seeds and fry for 30 seconds before adding the paste. Fry for a further minute then add the potatoes. Continue cooking until the potatoes have a good crust. Transfer to a dish with all the crispy bits of the spices and leave to cool. Season to taste, if necessary.

Combine the yoghurt, coriander, lime juice and zest and spoon over the potatoes just before serving.

Coconut lime tart

This surprisingly light lime tart can be prepared the day before, or even further in advance as it freezes well. The zingy lime gives it a refreshing flavour, while the coconut adds a slightly chewy texture. Serve with thick cream and fresh raspberries.

SERVES 10

400g (14oz) plain flour, plus extra for dusting

pinch of salt

200g (7oz) unsalted butter, chilled and cut into cubes

1 tbsp refined golden sugar

1 egg yolk

1 tsp vanilla extract

200g (7oz) desiccated coconut

juice of 2 limes, finely grated zest of 3 limes

3 tbsp rum

300 ml (10fl oz) double cream

3 medium eggs, lightly beaten

125g (4½oz) refined golden caster sugar

icing sugar, for dusting

Put the flour and salt in a food processor and whiz for a minute or two. Add the butter and process until the mixture resembles breadcrumbs. Add the sugar, egg yolk and vanilla extract and, with the motor running slowly, pour in a very small amount of chilled water until the mixture comes together in a ball. Wrap the ball in cling film and set aside to rest in the fridge for 10 minutes.

Roll out the dough on a well-floured surface until the pastry is 5mm (¼in) thick. Grease a 23cm (9in) loose-bottomed flan tin and line it with the pastry, pressing it down firmly. Set in the fridge for a further 20 minutes.

To make the filling, place the desiccated coconut, lime juice and zest, rum and cream in a blender and pulse together. Set aside for 15 minutes for the coconut to soften.

Preheat the oven to 200°C/400°F/Gas 6. In a clean bowl, whisk together the eggs and sugar until pale and light. Gradually add large spoonfuls of the coconut paste to the egg mixture, whisking until there are no lumps. Spoon this mixture into the pastry case and bake for 30 minutes until the tart is golden.

Sprinkle with icing sugar and heat the top with a blowtorch to finish or flash the tart under a grill until the top is caramelised.

Toffee, chocolate and oat squares

These extremely rich but moreish bites provide that indulgent sweetness for a picnic or any other occasion. They freeze brilliantly or will keep in airtight container in fridge for up to 10 days, so they can be made well in advance – if they don't get nibbled first!

SERVES 20

225g (8oz) plain flour

110g (4oz) porridge oats

150g (5½oz) soft light brown sugar

½ tsp bicarbonate of soda

½ tsp fine salt

150g (5½oz) unsalted butter, plus extra for the chocolate

1 egg, beaten

225g (8oz) dark chocolate

150ml (5fl oz) double cream

4 Mars bars, chopped into little pieces

Grease and line a Swiss roll tin with baking parchment. In a food processor, blend the flour, oats, sugar, bicarbonate of soda, salt and butter until the mixture is thick and pale. Slowly add the beaten egg, blending all the time. Press three-quarters of the mixture evenly into the prepared tin.

Break the chocolate into a microwaveable bowl, add a little butter and cook on High for 4 minutes, or in a heatproof bowl set over a pan of simmering water, and pour over the oat mixture, leaving a margin of 2.5cm (1in) around the edges. Freeze for 30 minutes.

Preheat the oven to 180°C/350°F/Gas 4. Bring the cream to the boil in a small pan, then lower the heat to simmering point. Tip in the pieces of Mars bars and stir until the sweets have melted and the mixture is smooth. Remove the frozen oat mix from the freezer and pour this caramelly cream over the frozen base. Crumble the remaining oat mixture on top and bake in the oven for about 25 minutes until golden. Allow to cool completely before cutting into squares.

Double chocolate brownies

American-style brownies are always extremely popular and are so easy to make. For the best brownies, have the oven at the exact temperature before you bake them, and be sure to follow the timings. (If anything, err on the side of having the brownies slightly undercooked for a delicious, more gooey texture.)

SERVES 24

125g (4½oz) dark chocolate

250g (9oz) unsalted butter, diced

4 eggs

400g (14oz) refined granulated sugar

115g (4oz) plain flour, sifted

1 tsp vanilla essence

60g (2oz) chopped walnuts

60g (2oz) good-quality white chocolate, roughly chopped

Preheat the oven to 200°C/400°F/Gas 6 and line a deep Swiss roll tin with greaseproof paper.

Break the chocolate into a microwaveable bowl, add the butter and cook on High for 4 minutes, or in a heatproof bowl set over a pan of simmering water, until melted. Set aside to cool to room temperature.

In a large bowl, beat together the eggs and sugar until thick and light coloured. Fold in the cooled melted chocolate, followed by the flour, vanilla, nuts and white chocolate. Pour the mixture into the prepared tin and bake for 25 minutes until the centre is semi-firm.

Remove from the oven, leave them to cool completely in the tin, then when cold turn them out onto board and cut into bite-sized squares.

Storecupboard Staples & Speedy Standbys

Entertaining friends should always be a pleasure, not a chore, and as much as I love cooking for my friends, if I've invited them over, I want to spend time with them. I find I get more chance to chat if I have part-prepared food in advance, or have some things on standby to cut down the cooking time or to serve to friends who unexpectedly arrive on my doorstep.

Whether it's nibbles to accompany drinks, a speedy snack, a languorous lunch or a decadent dinner, there are some accompaniments and extras I love to have to hand. Here, in this chapter are some of my favourite and most often used 'staples and standbys', which always save me at the last-minute or help to enliven an otherwise simple dish.

Roasted mixed spices

2 cinnamon sticks

50g (2oz) coriander seeds

50g (2oz) cumin seeds

50g (2oz) mustard seeds

50g (2oz) fenugreek seeds

50g (2oz) cloves

6 cardamom pods

I love the flavour that mixed spices can give to meat, and making your own blend means it is so much fresher and less musty than any bought version. Making a spice mix is easy if you use a small coffee/spice grinder – but you do need to keep it only for this purpose and this specific blend to avoid tainting other mixtures with these flavours. Once blended, the mix can be kept for up to 2 months in an airtight container stored in a cool dry place.

Put all the ingredients in a dry frying pan over a medium heat and cook until they begin to pop and are lightly toasted. Transfer to the grinder and pulse to form a fine mix. Use at once or transfer to an airtight container.

Bouquet garni

1 celery stick

sprig of fresh thyme

handful of parsley stems

1 bay leaf

These little packages are bursting with flavours and make a real difference to soups and stews, etc. Dried versions do not give half the flavour of a fresh one, and they are so easy to make; simply wrap the herbs together tightly with some sewing thread and drop them in!

Flavoured oils

Lemon oil

peel from 2 unwaxed lemons

Chilli oil

2 medium red chillies, halved, deseeded and finely sliced

Herb oil

large handful of fresh basil, rosemary, sage or thyme

pinch of sea salt

1 garlic clove

Garlic oil

8 garlic cloves, peeled and finely chopped

pinch of sea salt

Having flavoured oils to hand can instantly add colour and a unique flavour to a salad, fish, meat or other dishes without needing lots of ingredients and preparation.

All you need to do is warm 200ml (7fl oz) good-quality extra virgin olive oil in a saucepan with a lip, set it aside to cool to room temperature, then pour it over the chosen flavour and leave it to infuse. For herb oil put all the ingredients, including cold oil, in a blender and whizz until combined.

These oils should be stored in sterilised bottles and used within 3 days of making.

Oriental dressing

2 tbsp rice wine vinegar

2 tbsp light soy sauce

zest and juice of 2 limes

1 tbsp groundnut oil

1 tbsp refined caster sugar

1 garlic clove, grated

1 spring onion, finely chopped

small of bunch coriander, finely chopped

1 tbsp fresh mint leaves, finely chopped

Fresh, light and colourful, this delicious dressing contains a timeless combination of flavours.

Place all the ingredients in a screw-top jar and shake well to combine. This will keep in the fridge for up to a week.

Roasted cherry plum tomatoes

450g (1lb) red, yellow or orange cherry plum tomatoes

caster sugar, for sprinkling

sea salt and freshly ground black pepper

extra virgin olive oil

I like to buy my tomatoes three days before roasting, then I leave them out at room temperature to properly ripen. Once roasted they won't last long because they are so delicious and can be eaten at practically every meal!

Slice each tomato lengthways in half and spread them over a shallow baking tray lined with foil. Sprinkle with caster sugar, salt and pepper, then bake in very low oven (at about 100°C/200°F/Gas ¼) for 2 hours.

Store the cooled tomatoes in a clean, sterilised jar (washed once in the dishwasher and dried in an oven set to a low heat) and cover them with a layer of extra virgin olive oil.

These tomatoes can be stored in the fridge for a month.

Tomato chutney

SERVES 6

3 tbsp sunflower oil

¼ teaspoon black mustard seeds

¼ nigella seeds

¼ tsp fennel seeds

10 garlic cloves, chopped into large pieces

12 plum tomatoes, roughly chopped

1½ tsp ginger paste

1 tsp chilli powder

2 tsp sugar

½ tsp salt

2 green chillies, deseeded and finely chopped

We discovered this fantastic chutney while in India. The farm where we stayed near Nimaj, in Rajasthan, was owned by a family who cooked the best food we ate during our whole trip.

Heat the oil in a wok until hot, then add all the seeds and garlic and cook, stirring, for 2 minutes before adding the tomatoes.

Toss in the ginger paste and chilli powder and continue cooking until most of the liquid has evaporated. Add the sugar and cook until the oil leaves the sides of the pan.

Finally, stir in the salt and the green chillies. Serve warm.

Quick coriander and lime tartare sauce

SERVES 8

2 eggs, at room temperature

salt and freshly ground black pepper

2 garlic cloves, peeled

1 tsp mustard powder

250ml (8fl oz) sunflower oil

60ml (2fl oz) olive oil

2 tbsp lime juice

2 tbsp small capers, drained

6 small cornichons, finely chopped

2 tbsp chopped coriander

(this recipe includes raw egg, so do not serve it to vulnerable groups, such as pregnant women and old people)

The lime and coriander transform a classic tartare sauce into this more fragrant version. Serve with any fish or fish cakes.

Break the eggs into the blender, add salt, pepper, the garlic and mustard powder. Blend well.

Through the feeding tube, add the sunflower oil in a very slow but steady trickle. Once the eggs have emulsified to form a mayonnaise, add the olive oil and remaining ingredients. Check the seasoning and serve.

The sauce will keep, covered, in the fridge for a week.

Salsa verde

1 large bunch flatleaf parsley

1 bunch basil

14 mint leaves

2 anchovies, rinsed

2 garlic cloves, peeled

½ red onion, peeled and chopped

2 tsp capers, rinsed

3 tbsp red wine vinegar

1 tsp French mustard

175ml (6fl oz) extra virgin olive oil

This piquant, vibrant sauce can be made a day ahead and be kept, covered, in the fridge. It is perfect served as a canapé on Parmesan shortbread with a sprig of rocket and shaving of Parmesan. It also makes an ideal sauce over some grilled white fish, pink lamb fillet or veal chop.

Place all the ingredients in the food processor, apart from the oil, and blend. Slowly drizzle the oil into the mix with the motor running until it is blended. Check the seasoning and serve.

Caramelised shallot topping

2 onions, very finely sliced

15g (¾oz) butter

1½ tsp olive oil

1½ ground cinnamon

1 medium chilli, halved, seeded and finely sliced

salt and freshly ground black pepper

3 tsp soft brown sugar

good squeeze of lemon juice

small bunch of coriander and mint, roughly chopped

This is a unique topping for any potato-covered pie or meat with a creamy sauce. It not only gives a perfect finished look, but also gives a fresh spicy kick.

Fry the onions in the butter and oil over a medium heat until golden. Turn up the heat to brown the onions quickly. Add the cinnamon, chilli, salt, pepper and sugar. Continue to cook until the onions are slightly caramelised.

Squeeze over some lemon juice and add the chopped herbs. Set a large spoon of this topping over each serving.

Herb purée

75g (3oz) parsley

30g (1oz) butter

2 shallots, peeled and sliced

2 garlic cloves, finely grated

200g (7oz) spinach

100g (3½oz) mint

40g (1½oz) chervil

150ml (5fl oz) cream
salt and freshly ground black pepper

Delicious dolloped over some roast chicken, fish, scallops or veal chops.

Bring a pan of water to the boil, drop in the parsley just to blanch it, and refresh immediately under very cold water. Set aside to drain.

Heat the butter in a heavy frying pan, add the shallots and garlic and cook until soft. Add the spinach, mint and chervil and sauté until the leaves are just wilted.

Transfer to the liquidizer along with the parsley and cream and blitz for about 4 minutes or longer until totally smooth and a vibrant green. Season with salt and pepper.

Herb butters

5 tbsp fresh herbs

175g (6oz) butter

These make a perfect accompaniment to grilled fish, scallops, poultry, red meat or pasta. They are quick to put together and freeze really well when rolled into a sausage shape and wrapped in cling film.

The herb you use depends on the season, and whether you want to flavour meat or fish.

Anchovies also make a wonderful butter mixed with unsalted butter, lemon juice and chopped parsley.

Saffron aioli

2 pinches saffron threads

2 tbsp boiling water

2 egg yolks

3 garlic cloves, finely chopped

juice 1 lemon

splash of Tabasco

1 tsp Dijon mustard

1 tsp tomato purée

½ tsp sugar

300ml (10fl oz) sunflower oil

salt and freshly ground black pepper

(this recipe includes raw egg, so do not serve it to vulnerable groups, such as pregnant women and old people)

Perfect with a bowl of raw vegetables, chunky chips, in a hearty fish soup or stew, red pepper or tomato soup. Or just in a sandwich. There are too many uses to list...!

Do not use stainless steel cutlery when making or serving aioli, as it will give it a metallic flavour. Use a rubber spatula and silver/wooden spoon to serve.

To make the aioli, place the saffron in a small bowl. Poor over the water and leave for 5 minutes, to allow the colour and flavours to release.

Place the egg yolks, garlic, lemon juice, Tabasco – to taste – mustard, tomato purée and sugar in a blender. Slowly drizzle in the oil and blend to form a thick creamy mayonnaise.

Add the saffron with its liquid and season with salt and pepper to taste.

Roasted red onions

5 red onions, peeled and sliced

100g (3½oz) refined golden caster sugar

salt and freshly ground black pepper

100ml (3½fl oz) balsamic vinegar

60ml (2fl oz) extra virgin olive oil

I love to use these mixed with any cheese dish or salad. They are perfect as the topping for a bruschetta with anything from Gorgonzola to rare beef fillet. They will keep, covered, in the fridge for up to 3 weeks.

Preheat the oven to 180°C/375°F/ Gas 4.

Spread the onions over a foil-lined baking tray. Sprinkle with the sugar, salt, pepper, balsamic vinegar and olive oil. Toss well with your hands and roast in the oven for 45 minutes, stirring from time to time until they become a deep purple in colour.

Pastry

I always make my own pastry (apart from filo and puff pastry – Dorset and Saxby's do it so well and their versions contain no additives); it is much lighter and gives me the opportunity to add various different flavours. For instance, caster and muscovado sugars, cocoa powder, lemon zest, orange zest, almonds and hazelnuts for a sweet shortcrust, and Parmesan, mustard powder, cayenne pepper, finely chopped rosemary or fresh thyme for a savoury tart.

I prefer to use chilled unsalted butter for sweet pastry and often use frozen cubes in the heat of the summer. I add a pinch of sea salt and pepper to a savoury pastry.

Plain savoury shortcrust pastry

MAKES ENOUGH TO LINE A 28CM (11IN) DEEP, LOOSE-BOTTOMED TART TIN

300g (10oz) plain flour, plus extra to dust

pinch of sea salt

140g (5oz) salted butter, chilled and cubed

chilled water

Sift the flour and salt into a food processor and blend, to incorporate some air. Add the butter and blend until it forms fine breadcrumbs. With the motor running, slowly pour chilled water through the top of the machine until the dough just begins to form one large ball.

Remove the pastry from the machine, flatten it on a large plate and put it in the fridge for 20 minutes to rest. Roll it out on a cold (ideally granite/ marble) surface with plenty of flour to prevent the pastry sticking to the rolling pin or surface. Continue to roll, turning the pastry over until you have a circle large enough to fit the tin with some overhang.

Roll the pastry back over the top of the rolling pin and carefully set it into the tin. Press it well into all the contours of the tin and chill again for 20 minutes, to prevent it shrinking, before blind baking.

Orange mascarpone cream

MAKES ENOUGH TO SERVE 8

250ml (8fl oz) good crème fraîche

250ml (8fl oz) mascarpone

zest 1 large orange and 1 tbsp juice

1 tsp vanilla essence

The perfect accompaniment for any dessert, or as a filling for fruit tarts made with mixed fresh berries. It is also delicious as a filling for fresh profiteroles, drizzled with warm chocolate sauce.

In a large bowl, mix all the ingredients together and transfer to a pretty glass bowl to serve.

Index of recipes

Snowflake symbol indicates recipes
are suitable for freezing

Acknowledgements

I want to dedicate this book to my mother who early on taught me the enjoyment of cooking and delicious food; to my beloved daughters, Lucy and Eliza, who are following a similar path.

And to Charlie who, without his support and enthusiasm this book would simply have never been published!

My special thanks too to Andrew Barron who's kindness, help and encouragement have been wonderful in bringing this book about and to Helena Caldon who's dedicated eye and support have also been a true source of strength. To James Murphy who's astonishing professionalism and photography has lifted the book to another level. And finally, to Andrew Johnston who's friendship, support and knowledge of the publishing world has been invaluable.

First published in 2011 by Claire Caminada

Text © Claire Caminada 2011

Photography © James Murphy 2011

Claire Caminada has asserted her right to be identified as the author of this Work in accordance with the Copyright, Designs and Patents Act 1988

ISBN 978-0-9569793-0-8

Food photography by James Murphy
Food styling by Janet Smith
Edited by Helena Caldon
Designed by Andrew Barron

Colour origination by XY Digital
Printed and bound by 1010 Printing International Limited, China